9-3-90

LNWRTH
(VILL BKSHP)

D0845203

THE THREE-STAR BLITZ

THE THREE-STAR BLITZ

The Baedeker Raids and the start of Total War 1942–1943

CHARLES WHITING

LEO COOPER
LONDON

First published 1987 by Leo Cooper Ltd

Leo Cooper is an independent imprint of
the Heinemann Group of Publishers
10 Upper Grosvenor Street, London W1X 9PA
LONDON   MELBOURNE   JOHANNESBURG   AUCKLAND

ISBN 0-85052-881X

Printed in Great Britain by
Butler & Tanner Ltd, Frome and London

CONTENTS

ILLUSTRATIONS

1. Lübeck Cathedral.
2. The spire of Lübeck Cathedral collapses.
3. Victims of the raid on Lübeck.
4. St Martin's Church, Coney Street, York.
5. The Guildhall, York.
6. Wrecked convent in York.
7. Canterbury Cathedral after the raids.
8. Wrecked buildings in the St George's area of Canterbury.
9. St George's Church, Canterbury.
10. St George's Street, Canterbury.
11. The Wincarnis Works, Westwick Street, Norwich.
12. St Benedict's Gate, Norwich.
13. Exeter Cathedral.
14. Catherine Street, Exeter.
15. St Mary's R.C. Church, Bath.
16. Upper Bristol Road, Bath.
17. Cologne from cathedral tower.
18. American troops enter Cologne.
19. Bomb damage in Hamburg.
20. Airfields today: Tockwith; Long Marston; Pocklington.

The author and publishers are grateful to the following for permission to reproduce copyright photographs: *The Kentish Gazette*, Nos. 7, 8, 9 and 10; George Swain, Norwich, No.12; *The Express and Echo, Western Times and Gazette*, Nos. 13 and 14; *Wessex Newspapers*, Nos. 15 and 16; Associated Press, No.17; *Imperial War Museum*, No.19.

"We shall go all out to bomb every building in Britain marked with three stars in the Baedeker Guide."
Baron Gustav Braun von Sturm

INTRODUCTION

For me, of course, it had all been a bit of a lark. After nearly three years of waiting, when they finally came that early Wednesday morning in April, 1942, dropping their "Christmas tree" flares across the centre of the old city, it meant excitement, the start of a big adventure for an impressionable fifteen-year-old. Almost as soon as the sirens started, there were significant thuds all around and through the bedroom window I could see the unnatural glare of magnesium from the incendiaries burning on the roofs opposite. *This was it!*

My father, in his Home Guard uniform, was already in control, shepherding the neighbours inside the house (no one trusted the outside shelters—garden sheds with the window bricked up and an extra layer of concrete on the roof). Hurriedly, the women were shoved underneath the big kitchen table, while the men—my father, the neighbourhood warden (who had abandoned his post very smartish as soon as the first high explosive bomb dropped nearby) and I—stood guard. We'd all heard tales of Jerry parachutists being dropped during air raids.

In the event no *Fallschirmjäger* came winging down. Instead, the hot water boiler in the corner burst, spraying the ample bottom of the lady from next door with scalding water. "I've been hit," she shrieked, "I'm bleeding!", at the same instant as the kitchen door blew off.

My father was propelled by the rush of hot air from the kitchen into the next room, while soot came pouring down the chimney. The air raid warden began to blub and the fat lady's cries continued: "Won't anybody help me? *I'm bleeding to death!*" It was like a scene from an Ealing comedy. Later, after the Jerries had gone, I went outside to pick up shrapnel and spent bullets as souvenirs. I did not know till afterwards that 300 people had been killed or wounded that night and that one third of all homes had been damaged or destroyed. It was only later that I heard from a fellow fifth-former how he had watched our dead maths teacher being carried out of his wrecked flat on a door; from another, how he'd seen a delayed-action land mine explode the following morning and shower debris on a mother running with her pram. The little boy inside had been killed outright. But for me, however, that German Baedeker raid on the fourth English cathedral city to be attacked would remain, as I grew up, something of a comic adventure. A bit of a lark.

Three years later, as an eighteen-year-old soldier in an armoured column working its way through Cologne in pursuit of the retreating Germans, I realized that I had been an innocent eye-witness, in part, to a dreadful and permanent change in the nature of air warfare.

There was something awesome about this mile after mile of grey ruins. No sound save the clatter of our tracks and the distant rumbling of the permanent barrage. Miraculously the Cathedral spires still soared into the sky, but they served only to emphasize the two-dimensional rubble of the lunar landscape below.

What I was seeing was part of the retaliation for what had happened in York back in 1942. One month after my native city was raided, the RAF had launched its unprecedented 1,000-bomber attack on Cologne. Then for month after month, year after year, RAF Bomber Command, plus its ally, the US Eighth Air Force, had gone on and on bombing the Rhenish metropolis. Now, for the first time, I was seeing the result of unrestricted aerial warfare. Not that I felt any sympathy for the Germans; my own grandmother had been killed only the year before in London by their so-called revenge weapon, the V-2. In my simple mind, I thought they deserved it.

All the same, the sight of this devastated German city did shock me a little. As we clattered over the swaying pontoon bridge, I assumed that, with such damage, Cologne would never be rebuilt.[1] Thereafter, as the British Army advanced ever deeper into Northern Germany, I saw more and more cities as bad as Cologne—or even worse: Münster, Osnabrück, Bremen, Hamburg (where 70 per cent of the city had been destroyed, with 80,000 casualties, in a single week in 1943), and Lübeck, where it had all started back in 1942.

The realization grew that, at home in England, we had had not the slightest inkling of what those brave young men in blue (of whom 56,000 had been killed in action over the Continent) had done to Germany between 1942 and 1945. Systematically and according to plan, aided by their somewhat reluctant American allies, they had shattered one city after another; for it was the unstated intention of their masters to cause the wholesale destruction of German civilian morale by terror from the sky.

At the time, of course, the vast majority of us, on either side, were unaware of the plans of those who initiated this terrible new kind of warfare. What did we know of Hitler's hope to raze London to the ground by fire? Or Goering's plan to retaliate for the RAF's bombing of Lübeck and Rostock by raiding one undefended English cathedral city after another? How could we know, when the Germans employed their ultimate retaliation weapons, the V1 and the V2, that Winston Churchill would seriously propose using mustard gas against major German centres of population? In the summer of 1944, when the flying-bomb attacks on London were raising the death toll to the level of the 1940–41 blitzes, he wrote to the Chiefs-of-Staff:

> I want you to think very seriously over this question of using poison gas . . . It is absurd to consider morality on this topic when everybody used it in the last war without a word of complaint from the moralists or the Church. On the other hand, the bombing of open cities was regarded as forbidden. Now everybody does it as a matter of course. It is simply a question of fashion changing as she does between long and short skirts for women. . . . One really must not be bound within silly conventions of the mind, whether they be those that ruled in the last war or those in reverse which rule in this.[2]

In spite of the doubtful equation of comparing the use of mustard gas against troops with the use of it against civilians, who did not possess the soldiers' knowledge and equipment, most of our wartime generation would have judged Churchill to be right. But that 1944 memorandum did show that Britain, too, had now thrown public morality out of the window: "One really must not be bound within silly conventions." Nazi Germany had long dispensed with morality. Now it was Britain's turn. Soon it would be that of the United States. Hiroshima and Nagasaki would be the result.

The Three-Star Blitz is the story of the German attacks on a number of provincial English cathedral cities and other, smaller towns.

These raids were soon dubbed "the Baedeker raids", named after the German publisher Karl Baedeker, whose famous guidebooks to Europe's great cities first appeared in the nineteenth century.

What happened in those English cathedral cities back in 1942 started a dreadful chain reaction, which is still with us today. Thousands of innocent men, women and children are still suffering because of it.

Death and destruction from the air is with us to stay.

Many private individuals, in both Germany and Britain, have contributed to this book by sharing their memories with me. I would like to thank them collectively for their kind assistance.

I should also like to thank the editors of the *Hull Daily Mail, Yorkshire Evening Press, Bridlington Free Press, Eastern Counties Newspapers, Navy News, Western Daily Press, Norwich Mercury, Daily Mirror, Bath and Wells Chronicle and Herald,* and, last but not least, Radio Devon in Exeter. The yellowing clippings recording the long-forgotten little tragedies and heroic self-sacrifice of ordinary men, women and children in that terrible time were invaluable.

C. W.,
Wittlich, Germany,
Autumn, 1986

PART I

THE SOWING OF THE SEED

"I want fires everywhere. Thousands of them! Then they'll unite in one gigantic area conflagration. Goering has the right idea. Explosive bombs don't work, but it can be done with incendiary bombs—total destruction of London!"

Adolf Hitler, 1940

ONE

The day dawned crystal-clear, with a touch of snow in the air, and the wind blowing down the Baltic seemed to come straight from the North Pole. But it wasn't a bad day for shopping, as long as a person was warmly dressed and, in towns all over northern Germany, the streets were crowded with people. Tomorrow was Palm Sunday, the day on which Lutheran children were traditionally confirmed. Harassed *Patentanten*[1] were buying last-minute confirmation presents while mothers and older sisters stood patiently in the long queues outside butchers' shops, in the hope of securing a piece of pork for the *Schweinebraten*, the main attraction of tomorrow's celebration.

In Lübeck, the old Hansa port on the Baltic, which Thomas Mann, its most famous son, had put on the literary map with his novel *Buddenbrooks*, it was no different. Although most of the fathers and older brothers were away now, fighting on the *Ostfront* in Russia, many elderly guests were expected from the outlying villages and small towns to help celebrate the great day. Mothers were busy pressing the black suits their sons would wear on the morrow, ironing the girls' white blouses, checking the white gloves, the boys' bow-ties, the Bibles—all the hundred and one little tasks that mothers have to attend to on such occasions. Including, of course, the cooking.

Food might be in short supply, this third year of war, but of drink there was plenty. The régime well knew the value of alcohol as a palliative for morale-sapping fears which had been growing ever since the Wehrmacht marched into Russia the previous summer. The citizens of Lübeck were all too familiar with those black-framed

7

announcements, complete with Maltese Cross, announcing that Rifleman X or Tank Sergeant Y had died "for Folk, Fatherland and Führer". But there was *Korn* and *Kuemmel* enough to make one temporarily forget those who would never come back.

Meat was a different matter. Sugar and fats were scarce, too. Many a harassed mother had been saving for months now, carefully hoarding her coupons to ensure there would be the traditional *Braten* (roast) this Sunday, followed by the oversweet *Torten* (tarts) and *Puffer* (a kind of madeira cake) loved by the North Germans.

Some of these city dwellers had gone into animal husbandry in a small way, and many a flat balcony now accommodated unsuspecting rabbits and chickens which would be slaughtered soon for the roast. In the event, it was not just the animals that would be killed before the day was out.

Young Charles Coleman, with his strangely English-sounding name, was among those who would be confirmed on the morrow. "Although Father was called up and was away," he remembers forty years on, "our family intended to celebrate just as if this was peacetime."

> Already as the first cold rays of the winter sun began to sneak into our flat, my mother was busy with a fine roast which was bubbling and crackling away in the oven. She had been saving coupons to buy it for weeks. Indeed by afternoon my mother had begun to set the places in the "best room", which was only used on Sunday and high occasions, complete with silver and lace tablecloth. . . . Little did we know then that we would eat that roast long before Sunday was over and under very different circumstances than we had anticipated.[2]

Fifteen-year-old Ingrid Reiter, who lived not far away from Charles Coleman in the Kottwitzstrasse, was also looking forward to the best Sunday dinner she had eaten in many a week. Her aunt was already busy preparing a huge dish of *Rotkohl* (red cabbage, a north German speciality) complete with apple and goose fat, plus plenty of potatoes, and two splendid rabbits which she had "organized", as they called it then, on the black market. Like Charles, the girl could never have conceived where and under what circumstances she would finally eat those rabbits.

Heinz Hansen's crippled father (who had thus escaped the dreaded call-up for the *Ostfront*) had gone to even greater lengths to obtain a roast for his son's confirmation. The previous Friday night, accompanied by his wife, he had limped out into the countryside to a small farm he knew, where the farmer and his animals lived under the same roof in a timbered, red-brick farm typical of that part of the country. In the night air the two of them had negotiated. In the end a bundle of greasy Reichsmarks had changed hands; they had spat and slapped each other's palms in the traditional fashion, signifying that a deal had been arranged, and Herr Hansen had become the proud possessor of a plump suckling pig.

But how to take it back to Lübeck without being detected by the police? Black-market trading was severely punished; there was even talk of black-marketeers being sent to Neuengamme—a concentration camp outside Hamburg—and no one ever seemed to come back from there. But Herr Hansen had come prepared. Before the eyes of the amazed farmer, he fed the protesting pig a quarter of a litre of raw schnapps. It passed out like a light. Frau Hansen laid the unconscious pig in a high-sided wickerwork pram that she and her husband had brought with them. Then they wheeled the pig home through the blackout without even a second glance from the *Schupos* patrolling the streets. But as Heinz Hansen recalls today: "Poor Dad, after all his bother, never did manage to eat a piece of that pig—and he was so looking forward to it. That night he disappeared without trace, save for his surgical boot. That's all we ever did find of him."[3]

Indeed, apart from the few shortages, the war seemed very remote from Lübeck in this last week of March 1942. In the West, the whole of Europe from the Arctic Circle to the Mediterranean lay under the domination of Hitler. Only little England still held out. But since 1939 she had suffered defeat after defeat at the hands of the "Thousand Year Reich", and was not a power to be reckoned with.

Admittedly England did possess an Air Force; but since the war had begun three years before, Lübeck had had some 200 air raid warnings without a single bomb being dropped within the city limits. In any case, why would the Tommies want to bomb Lübeck? It was a target of little importance. There was the port, of course, through which strategic goods were shipped across the Baltic from Sweden. Officially Sweden was neutral, but the Swedes knew who was going to win the war and acted accordingly. There was the Dornier works, too, where they turned out flying boats for the German Navy, the Kriegsmarine. But that was about it. Lübeck remained a half-timbered, medieval town of some 180,000 people, its city centre filled with red-brick Gothic architectural treasures such as the great Marienkirche and the famous Dom, the cathedral. What purpose would it serve to bomb Lübeck?

Indeed, Berlin thought so little of the city's value as a strategic bombing target that there were only four heavy batteries and five light batteries to defend the whole place, perhaps twenty-odd guns in all. And, this very month, the High Command of the Luftwaffe had withdrawn the city's only searchlight unit and despatched it to the hard-pressed *Ostfront*.

"Later we would all say," Christa Hansen recalled, "that the Tommies attacked because they knew exactly how poorly Lübeck was defended. There were foreigners everywhere—Poles, Frenchmen, Belgians, Dutchmen—all working in the docks, and naturally the Swedish seamen came and went at will. We thought that the *Frendarbeiter* [foreign workers] had passed on the information about the state of our defences—or the lack of them—to some Swedish sailor who had been bribed to take it back to the British Secret Service which operated from Stockholm."[4]

But that was later. As the evening shadows started to steal over the Baltic, and here and there the first blackout curtains began to go up, the thought of an air raid on this North German backwater scarcely entered the minds of its citizens. The teenagers, sent early to bed, tossed and turned in their beds, thinking of the morrow and that solemn walk down the aisle, two by two in their dark confirmation suits, Bible in hand, to face the Herr Pfaffer in his long robe and ruff collar; then the party and the present-giving afterwards and the eating and the drinking.

Down below, in the kitchens, listening to the wireless—the *Volksempfanger* or "people's receiver" as it was called—on which one could not hear the lying propaganda of enemy stations, their mothers and aunts and elder sisters fussed over the food. Little did they know, these honest citizens of Lübeck, that for many of them this night would prove to be their last.

As the green flares rose into the night sky, the Wellingtons, with here and there an antiquated Blenheim, started to rattle along the tarmac on airfields throughout Yorkshire and East Anglia. One after another the lumbering planes, laden with bombs, sailed into the air. First a couple of score, then a hundred, now two hundred.

The crews watched their instruments anxiously as the heavily laden planes strained to achieve their ceiling of 15,000 feet. Now there were 234 of them airborne, crewed by sergeants who risked their necks nightly for fifteen shillings per day and officers who were paid the royal sum of twenty-nine shillings and ninepence for the privilege, young men in their twenties, mostly, of whom over a quarter would never see the end of the war.

The aircraft started to level out, flying in great V-shaped formations over the Vale of York and the fens of East Anglia. The steady hypnotic throb of the engines had its effect. The crews roused themselves from their individual cocoons. The gunners fired short bursts from their Brownings to test them. The skippers asked for a quick report on the intercom. There were the usual corny jokes about who was going to be "scared shitless" this night. But tonight, so the skippers reassured them, there was no need to be scared. For once they would not be flying over the "flak alley" of the Ruhr, where the deadly 88mms were massed solidly for mile after mile. Tonight they would be going in across the North Sea and then along the Baltic coast; they might even chance crossing the air space of "neutral" Sweden, knowing the Swedes would never fire at them in case they were Hun. Tonight it was going to be a piece of cake. The crews started to eat their sandwiches and unscrew their thermos flasks of coffee. It was going to be a long night.

They came in three flights. In the lead were ten Wellingtons, directed on to the target by the new secret weapon, a homing device known as "Gee". Later the German authorities asserted that the RAF bombers had turned off their engines and glided silently in from the Baltic. Hardly likely, but the Germans believed it! The leaders dropped marker flares for the second flight, forty fire-raisers armed with the huge 4,000lb bombs that RAF crews called "cookies", the standard weapon of the new generation of bombers coming into service.

In all, this RAF strike force would deliver 300 tons of bombs, 144 tons of that being a new kind of incendiary, which, when followed by the blast of high explosive, was calculated to fan into one tremendous blowtorch of flame that would consume the city. Fortunately for those at the receiving end, the notorious inaccuracy of the average RAF bomb-aimer would ensure that half the load, as the German authorities recorded later, "probably fell in the water".

It was eighteen minutes past eleven when the sirens sounded. As the startled Lübeckers tumbled from their beds, the first fire bombs fell on the town. These new incendiary bombs, which weighed 250lbs, were filled with a rubber mixture, petrol and an explosive charge: in essence, they were a primitive forerunner of the napalm bomb. The German Civil Defence organization had never encountered such bombs before. They showered down upon the city. One penetrated a four-storey building and struck an old deaf man who had not heard the alarm and was still fast asleep in his bed on the ground floor. Later he was found with the fire bomb which had not exploded, "literally riveting him to the bed, a round hole thirty centimetres in diameter punched in his frame by the English bomb".[5]

Soon the entire city centre was in flames. Fires in the timber-frame houses were too much for the local fire service; leaping from one wooden roof to another, the flames raced ahead of the hard-pressed firemen. Already the second alarm was beginning to wail, indicating that another wave of bombers was coming in.

"Ahead of the attack, a fiery parasite upon the body of a city began to writhe terribly into life," noted one of the second-wave pilots as they came in from the sea to drop their loads of high explosive bombs. "I saw the first flares, the target markers going down, the incendiaries budding, flowering, the short, bright blossoming of the bombs."[6]

Yorkshire navigator Harry Davidson, his lucky charm, a battered teddy bear, propped up in front of him on his tiny desk, was less poetically inclined:

> The whole bloody place was alight when we arrived. I'd never seen anything like it before and afterwards only Hamburg in '43 seemed to rival the intensity of the flames. As we came closer and the bomb-aimer started to sing out his instructions to the pilot—"steady, skipper, bit more to port, skipper" and all the rest of it—I forgot where I was and the danger we were in. I even forgot the flak and other shit which was winging our way. I was totally, completely fascinated by those flames below. The whole horizon was ablaze from end to end.[7]

One of the twelve planes lost on this raid blew up in a great balloon of fire. One wing went tumbling downwards, a giant gleaming sycamore leaf. No parachutes opened. But the pilots of the second wave, British and Polish (the latter had a personal score to pay off—Warsaw), fought their way through the flak and the turbulence caused by the exploding bomber, heading straight for the heart of the maelstrom.

*

Eighteen-year-old Gertrud Uecker had spent the evening watching the current heart-throb, the Dutch singing star Johannes Heesters, playing in the 1942 hit film *Man müsste Klavierspielen können* at the local Delta-Palast cinema. It was the last movie she would ever see. Just as she arrived home, the sirens began to sound—and a bomb landed on the house.

Half an hour later, Gertrud was struggling back to consciousness. Dizzy with shock and pain, she found she was half covered with débris. She wriggled free of the smouldering wreckage that had singed her dress, shaking her head to fight off the terrible pain and finding that somehow she could not see quite clearly. Then, as everything came into watery focus, she gasped with horror. Her mother lay among the shattered furniture, half-conscious and moaning with pain, most of her jaw ripped off. Next to her squatted Gertrud's younger brother, rocking back and forth, holding his left leg. A huge gaping wound had been torn in his calf. In the corner her elder brother lay motionless, bleeding from the head, face deathly pale, gasping for air with lungs that had collapsed with the force of the blast.

Gertrud struggled to her feet and took a look at her own body, the parts of it that appeared through the tattered frock. Her skin was covered with some kind of sticky goo which burned and itched. She tried to rub it away, but in vain, then touched her face and found it was covered with the same substance. Suddenly she felt a sharp pain in one eye. She looked at her hand with abruptly lop-sided vision, and gasped with horror: "My God . . . *I've pulled out my right eye!*"

Then she was stumbling into the burning street outside, screaming like a madwoman: "They're bleeding to death. They're bleeding to death in there."

Gertrud Uecker was not the only woman blinded that night as the HE bombs fell on Lübeck. Frau Hanna Gryzwatz—aged thirty-two and mother of three children, the eldest only five years old—found herself trapped by flames. Her house did not possess a cellar and she and her children had been sheltering in the living room. Four decades later her eldest son remembered:

> Surrounded by flames, my mother ran back and forth in the room like a frightened chicken, not knowing what to do. Suddenly she stopped in front of a huge glass-fronted cupboard full of her precious preserves, jams and the like, all filled into bottles and glass jars. In that very moment, there was a tremendous bang, which shook the whole house violently.

Outside a mine had exploded and our house had caught the full impact. I just caught sight of our pram, in which the six-week-old baby was lying, flying out of the room onto the balcony, when everything went black.

When I came to, I found myself outside as well. Together with my father, I staggered back into the shattered living room and helped to claw the smoking rubble from my mother. But it was already too late. Her whole body had been flayed and ripped apart by the flying glass from the cupboard and the jars it contained. Both her eyes had been ripped to shreds. She was blind for life.[8]

Meanwhile an elderly rescue-worker had found Gertrud Uecker running blindly through the streets, screaming hysterically with pain, for the pellets of phosphorus embedded everywhere in her half-naked body had started to smoulder and burn as they were exposed to oxygen. Gently but firmly, he made her lie down. Then, fighting off her flailing hands, he wrapped her tortured body in a sheet, picked her up and carried her to the South Hospital. Dr Karl Petersen, the thirty-four-year-old head surgeon at South Hospital, and his team of eight assistants were working flat out as casualties flooded in from all sides.

Young Gertrud was naturally treated as a priority case. But even as Dr Petersen bent over her, he knew that there was little he could do for her. Her life might be saved, but not her sight. After scores of operations Gertrud lost her left eye, too. But, like Frau Hanna Gryzwatz, she survived, alive, but blind.

That night Dr Petersen would excise eighteen eyes from women who had been hit during the raid, adding to the total of 180 German women who were blinded by enemy action during the course of the war. But, horrible as this was, Dr Petersen found that the true horror of that night lay in the hospital basement, which became known as "the body cellar". During a pause in his operations on the air-raid victims, Petersen went to see what was going on:

> There was no time to place the hundreds of new dead down there with any kind of dignity. They were simply tossed into the cellar by the rescue workers, all mixed up, a mess of bloody shattered limbs so that they presented a ghastly picture of death which I will never forget to the day I die.[9]

The city centre was ablaze. Adding to the chaos and confusion, when the bombers had released their loads they swooped low to blast away at the harassed firemen with their machine guns. The situation was bad enough as it was. The fires were out of control, the flames reaching so high that they could be seen in Hamburg, fifty miles away to the south, and some of the fires would continue to burn for two days, as the local authorities desperately appealed to surrounding towns to send all the help they could. Lübeck could cope no more.

Already panic had set in. The normally imperturbable North Germans, known for their phlegmatic nature, were now seized by a kind of mass hysteria. They threw caution to the winds. Grabbing whatever personal belongings they could find, covering their heads with pans or wrapping themselves in mattresses as protection against the shrapnel cutting through the air, they began to flee from the burning city.

Young Charles Coleman rescued what he could find of tomorrow's roast from the smoking ruins and wolfed it down, ash and all. A seven-year-old, whose mother had been killed, found himself buried under three metres of glowing rubble. Somehow he extracted himself and, finding a tin bath, held it over his head for protection. He survived.

From all over the city came reports of people trapped by the flames. One fire-section chief, Reinhard Flemke, recorded in his report after the attack:

> We burrowed deep into the rubble for some trapped people, using our hands, empty cans, even a large metal washing-up bowl . . . First we came across the charred skull of one victim and then a huge dead man, all of one hundred kilos, with immediately beneath him another man, still alive and buried up to his neck in rubble.[10]

What could they do? In the end they managed to tie a rope around the stomach of the dead man and, with a winch-and-tackle, began to heave him out until the victim started to scream, "Stop, stop, he's crushing my skull!"

So they left the man there for the time being—he turned out to be a soldier on leave from the Russian front—up to his neck in rubble, with another three dead or dying below him, while above him the grotesque corpse, suspended in mid-air, swayed back and forth.

The hard-pressed rescue services were hampered at every turn. Gas and electricity supplies had been cut off. The supply of drinking water gave out. As the flames sent temperatures soaring, the firemen and wardens gasped in vain for water to quench their thirst. Some broke into inns and looted whatever they could find. That night some firemen, so it was recorded, drank ten or twelve litres of strong local beer—and never felt a thing!

But at last the authorities could start counting the damage. 1,398 public buildings had been destroyed or damaged, and 58% of private houses had suffered a similar fate, as had 38% of private flats.

The docks, which should have been the primary target, together with the Dornier works, were virtually unscathed; they were working as normal within a few days. As one English eyewitness, A. G. Dickens, wrote after the war, "One third of the ancient city centre, isolated amid its canals, was destroyed . . . The docks and the industrial belt, ostensibly our real targets, seemed almost untouched by this rather unsuccessful raid of the pre-precision age of bombing."[11] But, unbeknown to Dickens, these civilian targets had been *deliberately* selected three years earlier.

The raid had destroyed the heart of Lübeck's *Altstadt*, the old city, the patrician residences of the eighteenth-century burghers. Churches such as St Marien, St Petri and the Cathedral itself had suffered extensive damage. It seemed as if the British had gone out of their way to destroy the cultural heritage of centuries.

Of course the local authorities were more concerned about the cost in human life, and the list of casualties was tragically long. Back in 1940, when the RAF had raided German land targets for the first time by bombing the Rhenish city of München-Gladbach, there had been only one casualty: surprisingly enough an Englishwoman living in Germany, killed by the bombs of her own countrymen. But after the raid on Lübeck that night in March, 1942, 320 people had died, including one Polish forced labourer and two Jewish citizens who had somehow managed to escape the holocaust so far. The oldest victim was a man in his eighties, the youngest a baby barely eight hours old, a victim of smoke poisoning. In addition, another 400 people had been badly injured and 14,000 rendered homeless. In nearly three years of war, this was the greatest blood-letting that the German civilian population had suffered so far. Overnight Lübeck became the worst-hit city in the whole of the Reich.

Immediately the German propaganda machine went into action, to attract sympathy and to hide the fact that local morale had been seriously damaged. As Fire Chief Lieutenant Dr Hans Bunswig stated, "The population is fully apathetic and attempting only to rescue their possessions."[12] Or as Hamburg fire officer First

Lieutenant Jacobs put it, "The whole population is in shock. . . . They are not capable of helping themselves."[13] Public collections for "the suffering citizens of Lübeck" were made in Paris. In Hamburg they struck a medal to commemorate the disaster. The Dutch Nazi Party sent a delegation of sympathy. In Copenhagen Professor Dr Schroeder thundered against the British: "Oran, Paris, Münster—now Lübeck! What barbarism! My anger against this scum of the Aryan world knows no bounds!"[14]

But in Berlin the Minister of Popular Enlightenment and Propaganda Dr Josef Goebbels, known behind his back as "the Poison Dwarf", was realist enough to acknowledge the truth in his diary:

> This Sunday had been thoroughly spoiled by an exceptionally heavy raid by the RAF on Lübeck. In the morning I received a very alarming report from our propaganda office there which I first assumed to be exaggerated. In the course of the evening, however, I was informed of the seriousness of the situation by a long-distance call from Kaufmann [the *gauleiter* of Hamburg]. He believes that no German city ever before has been attacked so severely from the air. Conditions in parts of Lübeck are chaotic.[15]

Four days later Goebbels confided to his diary:

> The damage [in Lübeck] is really enormous. I have been shown a newsreel of the destruction. It is horrible. One can well imagine how such awful bombing affects the population. Thank God it is a North German population, which on the whole is much tougher than the Germans in the south or south-east. Nevertheless we can't get away from the fact that the English air raids have increased in scope and importance. If they can be continued for weeks on these lines, they might conceivably have a demoralizing effect on the population.[16]

For all his vanity and intellectual pretensions, Goebbels was also a supreme realist, perhaps the only one in the whole bunch of pompous middle-class Brownshirts who ruled Germany in the 1940s. He knew that something had to be done to stop any further raids of this kind—and it had to be done *soon*.

TWO

On the last Sunday of December, 1940, the Germans had come to London yet again—over 500 bombers. For the last four months they had been attacking continuously, night after night. Some 30,000 Londoners had been killed, twice that number seriously injured, and half a million citizens had been made homeless. Now they were attacking again, as if they were determined to wipe the capital of the hated enemy off the map for good.

St Paul's Cathedral was ringed with flame. The City was ablaze from Moorgate to Aldersgate and from Old Street to Cannon Street. The Guildhall had already disappeared into the inferno. Railway stations were swamped in flames or falling rubble. By morning there would not be a single train running within miles of Central London; every station would be knocked out. London, so it seemed, was dying.

As the last of the attackers finally droned southward, leaving behind them 1,500 fires raging and another 700 Londoners dead or seriously injured, a stocky, broad-faced figure wearing the uniform of an Air Vice-Marshal thought he had seen enough. From his position on the roof of the Air Ministry building, it seemed that the whole of London was a sea of flames. He could see at least eight Wren churches burning.

Passionately angry, he decided that his chief ought to see what the Hun had done to London and went inside to fetch Air Chief Marshal Sir Charles Portal. Within minutes he was back out on the roof with the aristocratic, beak-nosed head of the RAF. For a while both men, wrapped in the cocoon of their own thoughts, stared at the terrible sight; then the Air Vice-Marshal broke the silence. "Well," he snapped to Portal, "they are sowing the wind."[1]

A year later, in February, 1942, Portal's companion had become head of Bomber Command, the only real offensive weapon which Britain possessed in that bitter winter of defeat. His name was Arthur "Bert" Harris, soon to be known to his crews as "Butcher" or "Bomber" Harris.

The new commander of the bomber strike force had come up the hard way. Packed off to Africa at the age of sixteen with five pounds in his pocket, he had attempted to make his fortune in farming, gold mining, driving horse teams. But the First World War had put an end to his attempts to become a millionaire. Enlisting in the Rhodesia Regiment, he had fought the Germans and their Boer allies up and down East Africa, "living on biscuits which you had to bust with your rifle butt, and bully beef which in that climate was almost liquid in the can".[2]

But it wasn't the food that turned the young bugler against the infantry; it was the marching. "How we marched! We marched and we marched and we marched, and, God knows, as far as I was concerned I'd already marched too far!"[3] Thus, as soon as the East African campaign was over and the Hun beaten, young Harris returned to England and volunteered for a new branch of the Armed Forces where he hoped he would never have to march another step—the Royal Flying Corps.

In the years that followed Harris saw action over England and France, and then, after the war, in India and various other parts of the Empire, where a cost-conscious War Office tended to use aircraft to bomb rebellious natives into submission rather than launch a full-scale campaign against them. Thus Harris learned his handiwork in the relentless school of colonial warfare, far away from the tut-tutting moralizers, the "bleeding hearts" and "parlour pinks" of the Old Country.

A forthright, sometimes abrasive man who was no respecter of persons, Harris progressed up the ladder of promotion, oblivious of the toes he trod upon in the process. On the outbreak of the Second World War he was appointed commander of the 5th Bomber Group and soon turned it into the best of the aerial strike forces—this at a time when there were strict instructions from the Air Ministry "not to bomb private property" and when air warfare seemed to consist of dropping leaflets on the enemy.

Now, two years later, Harris had the job he had been after all the time, the head of Bomber Command, the one force in the whole of the Armed Forces—so he thought, at least—which was capable of winning the war quickly.

Bomber Harris had come along at exactly the right time. In February, 1942, Britain's fortunes were at their lowest ebb. Singapore had just surrendered to the Japanese and the whole of the Far Eastern Empire had vanished. In the West Britain had suffered defeat after defeat, causing Churchill to wring his hands and exclaim, "Will they [British troops] *never* fight?" The U-boat campaign had reached such an intensity that starvation loomed ahead if something were not done soon.

In high places desperate measures were being considered. Publicly Churchill would soon announce that he would not hesitate to use poison gas if the Germans did so first. Privately he ordered that tests should be carried out immediately on the possibility of using anthrax against the enemy. To make matters worse, both America and Russia, now Britain's ally, were demanding that the Western Allies should invade France in 1942, and their demands were echoed by the local Communists and their fellow travellers. For suddenly these left-wingers, who had refused to support a "capitalists' war", had now become, since the invasion of Russia the previous June, the most fervent advocates of attack. "*Help Uncle Joe!*"—the slogan was scrawled everywhere, turning that ruthless mass-murderer Stalin into an avuncular, pipe-smoking, lovable old buffer.

"*Second Front Now!*", another slogan that was appearing on walls and bridges all over the nation this winter, was much more worrying to Churchill. He and his generals knew it was far too soon to launch an attack on Fortress Europe; the Army simply wasn't ready for an invasion of such magnitude.

Now, however, Churchill saw a way out, a means of striking back at the enemy and convincing both the Americans and the Russians that the British meant business. The nucleus of the idea had come in the shape of a report from Churchill's principal scientific adviser, Lord Cherwell, who had been born in Baden-Baden as Franz Lindemann. Over the winter of 1941/42 the RAF had been studying the effects of German bombing on the hard-pressed Yorkshire port of Hull, which, because it was the key port for supplying Russia, had continued to be attacked long after the bombing of London had ceased. The RAF investigators had estimated that, for every ton of bombs dropped on Hull, some 20–40 buildings had been demolished and 100–200 people rendered homeless. Cherwell's attention had been drawn to these statistics and, one month after Harris had taken up his appointment, he forwarded a report to Churchill stating that:

> Investigation seems to show that having one's house demolished is most damaging to morale. People seem to mind it more than having their friends or even relatives killed. At Hull signs of strain were evident, though only one tenth of the houses were demolished.[4]

Lord Cherwell, this bitter, German-born enemy of the Germans, thought, as did others at the top, that the way to pay back the enemy was to bomb civilian housing as the Germans had done in Hull, where only eight percent of the buildings were still undamaged and 146,000 people had been rendered homeless. Cherwell calculated that each British bomber had a life-span of fourteen operational missions; and if each bomber dropped three tons of bombs on a built-up area on each mission, it would, before it was finally shot down, make some 4,000 to 8,000 German civilians homeless. This would have a disastrous effect on the enemy war industry and morale. As he wrote to Churchill, "There seems little doubt that this would break the spirit of the people."[5]

Sir Archibald Sinclair, the Minister for Air, agreed with Cherwell. He found the latter's argument "simple, clear and convincing". He wasn't alone. There were plenty of hawks at the top who believed the Hun should be squeezed "till the pips squeak". Geoffrey Shakespeare, the Liberal MP for Norwich, wrote in a letter to Churchill:

> I am all for the bombing of working-class areas of German cities. I am Cromwellian—I believe in "slaying in the name of the Lord"—because I do not believe you will ever bring home to the civil population of Germany the horrors of war until they have been tested in this way.[6]

Mr Shakespeare would live to regret those words when his own constituency bore the brunt of the Germans' revenge.

Harris had once been stopped while driving his large American car at reckless speed and told by a young constable that he "might kill somebody" if he continued like this. Tartly Harris had replied, "Young man, I kill thousands of people every night!"[7] Now this hard, unfeeling man, who throughout the war never once visited any of his active-service stations to see his crews off before an "op", decided he would apply the new "de-housing" strategy advocated by Cherwell to the bombing of Germany.

By now Harris knew the chief weakness of his bomber crews— they were not very accurate. As one pilot remarked: "In those days [1941] we were lucky to find the town to be bombed—but actually to hit the target was little short of a frigging miracle!"[8] They were brave enough, but when they did encounter heavy anti-aircraft fire too many of them would deliberately jettison their bombs short of the target. And after several missions over the massed guns of the German flak alleys of the Ruhr, Hamburg, Berlin and the like, nerves began to fray and break. Already some ten percent of his crews were having their records stamped in red "LMF" (Lack of Moral Fibre) and were posted to the Army, to the RAF psychiatric hospital at Matlock, or to what was little better than a detention barracks at Sheffield.

What Harris needed was an easy target: one that could be easily located and easily bombed; and one that would give the most spectacular results for the smallest loss of life. He found it in Lübeck. The old Hansa port presented no location problems as it was on the Baltic coast. There were no flak alleys to cross and the place itself was lightly defended. Moreover, the city centre was like a tinderbox, filled with highly inflammable half-timbered houses. As Harris put it, "Lübeck was built more like a fire-lighter than a human habitation." With characteristic bluntness he added later, "I wanted my crews to be well blooded, as they say in fox-hunting, to have a taste of success for a change."[9]

In the event Harris's crews were well and truly blooded and they did enjoy a great deal of success. For the loss of a handful of bombers, less than five percent of the force, civilian morale in Lübeck had been dealt a serious blow. Now Harris wondered what his next "easy" target might be, gloating over the top-secret folder that contained his thirty-eight prime targets, which he would soon routinely pull out to bore important visitors with the statistics of bombs dropped, casualties caused, damage done.

Churchill did not believe that Harris's bomber offensive alone would bring the Germans to their knees. He could not share the easy optimism of a man whom he did not particularly like, although they were soon to appear on terms of apparent intimacy, dining regularly with each other. Indeed, Churchill would hastily distance himself from Harris once the war in Europe was nearing an end, and Harris would be forgotten, languishing in a kind of bitter voluntary exile in Rhodesia to the day he died.

But Churchill knew he needed Harris at this nadir of the war when even his own political future was at stake. If Harris's new campaign met with even moderate success, it would not only rally the war-weary civilians at home, it would also show the Allies—the Americans in particular (Churchill knew it was the Americans who would eventually win the war for him with their massive industry and overwhelming numbers)—that Britain was really fighting back. So he gave his approval to Harris's new bomber offensive. At a tolerable cost in British lives, the embattled island would be shown to be doing *something*. In the end it cost 56,000 young lives to do so.

Unaware of Churchill's attitude and flushed with his first victory, Harris attacked again. Once more his target was an easy one, the Mecklenburg port of Rostock. All the ingredients were the same as before: like Lübeck Rostock lay on the Baltic coast, a tinderbox of medieval half-timbered houses with minimal defences. And, again like Lübeck, Rostock suffered terrible damage as the ensuing firestorm swept through the old city.

"Community life in Rostock is almost at an end," Goebbels wrote in his diary.[10] For its part, the British Ministry of Economic Warfare stated: "It seems little exaggeration to say that Rostock has for the time being ceased to exist as a going concern."[11]

Now Harris rang the changes. In one of the most brilliantly executed raids of the war, the new four-engined Lancaster bomber was employed in a daring low-level daylight raid against the MAN engineering works at Augsburg. Twelve Lancasters surged in at 250 mph, virtually at roof-top height, or so it seemed to the terrified locals, and dropped their bombs on the MAN factory. Seven planes were shot down, five damaged and of the seventeen bombs only twelve exploded. The attack badly damaged the main tool shops but only kept them out of production for a short while. But the propaganda effect of this startling new RAF tactic (up to now they had only bombed at night) and of these gigantic four-engined bombers was tremendous. Not only in Britain, where its leader received the Victoria Cross and the surviving crews were showered with medals, but in Germany too.

The secret reports filed by the *Sicherheitsdienst*, the Security Service of the Gestapo, are full of the anger and astonishment felt by Augsburg's citizens that the RAF could carry out such an operation in "the home of the Messerschmitt fighter". As one report noted:

> The citizens [of Augsburg] were caught totally by surprise when the sirens sounded. They did not think it possible that the English would attack by daylight. The police had the greatest

23

difficulty in persuading them to go into the shelters . . . The mood was instantly low as they discovered that the Tommies dare attack so deep into the territory of the Reich without a fighter escort. . . . They felt it was disgraceful that they dare attack a city famed throughout the world for its production of fighter planes. They felt too that the flak defences were inadequate.

According to another report, it had been a poorly kept secret that Augsburg was a centre for the shipment of supplies to the Eastern Front. Consequently, many people felt that "the English attack was due to treachery. Someone had talked!"

A third report would have made heartwarming reading for Harris and his crews:

Everyone here is full of admiration for the boldness of the English pilots. They displayed great elan. Their precision bombing was widely praised and the fact that they came in at five hundred metres, hitting their targets with amazing accuracy. The admiration of the local populace was further increased by the fact that on the following day the English press gave no details of the raid. This caused, too, ugly rumours about the extent of the damage to Augsburg and the number of casualties.[12]

The Augsburg raid was the last straw as far as Hitler was concerned. Only a month before, he had been on the point of ordering an all-out attack on Britain by Goering's Luftwaffe after the raid on Boulogne—Billancourt, where the French casualties had amounted to 400 dead, with another 600 dead and 1,000 seriously wounded in the Paris area. He had felt that the French, even the loyal ones under Marshal Pétain—who had declared the day of the victims' funerals a day of national mourning—would begin to lose faith in Germany's mission if the Reich could not protect its subjects.

At the time the Führer's advisers had persuaded him against such a course. They had put the difficulties to him: that two-thirds of the crews in training in the west had had no combat experience; that their planes, dating back to the days of the Spanish Civil War, were already out-dated; and that the "old hares", the veterans, were now mainly engaged in training the "greenbeaks", as the raw recruits from the Reich were called.

Now, however, Hitler could not be restrained. Preoccupied as he was with the campaign in Russia, and remote as he was from his people (unlike Churchill, he never once visited a bombed German city throughout the war), he still knew that he might well lose the propaganda war if he did not retaliate. Although his crews in the west were mostly inexperienced, although the Luftwaffe was already fully committed in Russia, he gave the order—Britain must be attacked!

The problem was handed to the head of the Luftwaffe, "Marshal of the Empire" Hermann Goering. The World War One ace had been falling from favour for years now. Once he had proudly declared that if one single British plane ever bombed Germany then the people could call him "Meier" (presumably a Jewish name). Now British planes had been regularly bombing Germany for two years and "Fat Hermann" or "Fatty" (*der Dicke*), as he was known behind his back, had become a figure of fun. It was not surprising. He designed his own uniforms, which he changed up to twenty times a day. He wore rouge and painted his nails. He snorted cocaine through a jewelled tube and often when he talked to his subordinates, most of whom disliked their chief intensely, he ran gems in and out of his plump beringed fingers like a Greek might play with his worry beads.

Goering now found himself in a quandary. How was he to carry out the Führer's command? Where could he attack? Since the blitzes of 1940–41, most of Britain's major cities were effectively defended by massed guns and a barrage balloon system. His "greenbeaks" had neither the skill nor even, in some cases, the courage of their predecessors to brave such defences. London, Plymouth, Bristol and the like were, therefore, out of the question.

Milch, half-Jewish and an implacable enemy of Britain, his Inspector-General, thought he had the answer. The officer of whom one of his subordinates commented, "When Milch pisses, ice comes out", suggested that the Luftwaffe should take a leaf out of the Tommies' book. The staff planners should look for English equivalents to Lübeck and Rostock, cities that were lightly defended, easily accessible from Luftwaffe bases in France, and which, like the two Baltic ports, would burn like tinderboxes once they were hit by the lethal new combination of high explosive and incendiaries. Slowly the concept of what were to be known as the "Baedeker raids" was fashioned.

It started inauspiciously enough. One afternoon in early April, 1942, four Me 109s dropped suddenly out of the sky over Torquay, home of genteel maiden ladies and retired military gentlemen. The fighter-bombers came racing in from the sea at 150 feet, machine guns chattering, angry red flames rippling the length of their wings. The bewildered onlookers on the promenade had barely realized what was happening before the four planes had dropped their bombs and were scuttling back to the safety of their French bases.

In London no one took any notice of the minor raid on Torquay. The place had no military value whatsoever. There might, in due course, be indignant letters to *The Times* complaining about the local lack of defences. Some elderly ladies might now be in shock. But that was about the sum of it.

Four days later the German fighter-bombers made another of these seemingly senseless raids, this time on Brixham, just around the bay from Torquay. A week later they struck another coastal resort favoured by genteel elderly people, Bognor Regis, where King George V refused to be taken for his last cure; *"Bugger Bognor!"* are reputedly the last words he uttered. Then Swanage was hit, not once but twice, on consecutive days, and the following day it was Portland's turn.

Intelligence was puzzled. The Joint Intelligence Committee had predicted at the beginning of the year that "The tactics of the German Air Force against the British Isles are unlikely to differ materially from those experienced during the latter half of 1941."[13] What were the Intelligence experts to make of these new daylight raids which the Press was now calling "tip-and-run" attacks?

By the third week of April Exmouth, Bexhill, Folkestone, Hastings, Lydd, Dungeness, Cowes and Newhaven had all been attacked by these fast fighter-bombers, which seemingly didn't aim at any specific target but simply dropped their bombs—"tipped" these unimportant coastal towns and then "ran" for it.

One eye-witness of these tip-and-run raids, who was more concerned than most about German intentions, chanced to visit one of those coastal towns that April. Afterwards he described the scene as one of idyllic calm: sunshine warmed those strolling along the front while "the undertow rolled the pebbles on the foreshore with a gentle murmur and the gulls wheeled and shrieked as they had done in peace-time". Suddenly the calm was shattered. Roaring in from across the Channel,

> almost skimming the surface of the water, came two or three aircraft racing towards the shore with all their guns blazing. Shells tore at the promenade and shattered the Regency houses, the planes banked steeply and were gone before the AA gunners could even bring their weapons to bear. From the

streets at the back of the town, by the gasworks and the railway station, there came the sound of the bombs falling. The enemy was gone, racing out to sea again as the sirens sounded behind them a belated warning.[14]

The observer of this scene and of the failure of his gunners to react in time was General Frederick Pile, head of AA Command.

Pile, a hook-nosed little Irishman, had served for over thirty years in the Royal Artillery. Back in 1937, as a general on half pay, he had been brought back to take over the 1st AA Division, the first to be created as the threat of war between Britain and Germany began to loom large. To his consternation Pile found that the Division existed in name only. Apart from a few regulars, it consisted of untrained "terriers" who possessed only a handful of anti-aircraft guns, mostly antiquated models dating from 1918 and capable only of tackling Zeppelins. Indeed, the total number of guns then available to defend the whole of the United Kingdom was 146; even back in 1923, when thoughts of war had been furthest from the public mind, it was estimated that twice that number would be needed to defend London alone.

Undeterred, Pile had set to work in his usual forceful manner, prepared to fight not only the German enemy but the apathy of the British public, as well as the active opposition of those politicians, mostly left-wing, who did not believe in "wasting" public money on defence. The 1938 crisis helped a little. Money started to become available for defence and suddenly Pile, still trying to make his 1st Division effective, found himself commanding a whole corps—at least on paper. Later he wrote:

> Not that anyone who was given an appointment in connection with AA could fail to observe what a terrible state the air defence of the country was in after years of Treasury neglect and public apathy. We were all appalled at the fool's paradise in which the people of this country were living and particularly the people in London.[15]

Some 80,000 British men, women and children would pay with their lives for this lack of foresight.

Pile faced obstacles at every turn. Factories, right up to March, 1945, could not produce the time-fuses his shells needed, and, even then, with six weeks of the war to go, they were in short supply. Local councils wanted his guns moved because they "attracted" the bombers or cracked the toilet bowls in their council estates.

27

Throughout, he suffered from a chronic shortage of the right type of human material to man his guns. Four months after the war started, Christmas, 1939, Pile inspected a typical new intake to one of his frontline batteries:

> Out of twenty-five who arrived ... one had a withered arm, one was mentally deficient, one had no thumbs, one had a glass eye which fell out whenever he doubled to the guns, and two were in the advanced and more obvious stages of venereal disease.[16]

When, in 1942, the quality of manpower which was drafted to AA Command improved slightly, he was hampered in setting up mixed batteries because the ladies of the ATS objected to their girls working with men on moral grounds. Some of his conscripted Home Guards simply failed to turn up for duty.

Pile was forced to make do with whatever weapons he could find. Once, during a threatened German invasion, his men were so short of rifles that they had to be armed with pick-axe handles and medieval pikes; Pile became so despondent that he ordered his gunners not to speak about it, in case they alarmed the general public. On another occasion, in order to increase his gunners' efficiency, he said that £10 (a large sum in those days) would be awarded to those gunners most proficient in the recognition of enemy aircraft. When it came to handing over the money to the happy winners, the War Office refused to fund the venture and Pile had to pay out of his own pocket!

And yet, despite all the difficulties, Pile managed to cover the major areas of attack with his guns, barrage balloons and search-lights. Then, in April 1942, the Germans launched their seemingly purposeless tip-and-run raids, striking at ports and cities which were virtually undefended. A whole new area of defence had been opened up for AA Command, whose resources were already stretched to the limit.

Suddenly, as Pile was wondering how to deal with this new form of attack, the Germans struck again—this time by night, for the first time in over a year. Like everyone else, Pile was puzzled by the new German tactics. Where would they strike next, and when? Would an already harassed chief of AA Command be justified in removing his defences from London or Bristol to defend the new objectives, wherever they might be? For his resources were strictly limited. It was always the same story, as he wrote after the war:

> The supply of equipment was never sufficient for success until great damage had been done. The fact that the British always

28

win the last battle—and pride themselves on the fact, as if in some way it were more creditable than winning decisively at the first encounter and saving a lot of lives, time, trouble and expense—was largely the outcome of this supply position. We could not win the first battle because we were never ready, and so we made a virtue of necessity and drew what comfort we could from the cliché.[17]

The cost of such typical British apathy was high. In the next three months some 2,000 men, women and children were killed, three times that number injured, and the centres of some of the country's finest and oldest cities vanished for ever. In the event, Britain did indeed win the final battle in 1945 but, in the spring of 1942, she lost the Battle of the Baedeker Raids.

THREE

At the beginning of the war, back in September, 1939, it had all been rather exciting: the call-up, rationing, the first air-raid sirens, the flood of evacuees, the blackout. A few months later there had been Dunkirk: "Bloody marvellous!" the *Daily Mirror* had head-lined its account of the evacuation, the first British paper ever to print a profanity. Then a new man was at the helm, Winston Churchill, rallying the nation with that sonorous declamation of his: "We shall fight in the fields and in the streets, we shall fight in the hills; we shall never surrender!"

But nothing happened. The Huns never came and the fighting was in foreign fields and streets and hills. In one sense, of course, the war was ever-present: it was the sole topic of the newspapers, of the BBC, and of Movietone News, in which Bob Danvers-Walker talked of "knocking the Hun for six" and "whacking the Wop", as if the war were a game of cricket.

To most people war meant shortages. That spring a week's butter ration was about the same as we might smear on a single slice of toast today, bacon one good rasher a week and sweets four ounces a week. Rubbery dried egg and dehydrated potatoes from America filled the gap. The Ministry of Food advised strange recipes such as Trench Meat Pudding, Snoek Piquante and All Clear Sandwiches, which required no meat and gave plenty of bulk. Even tea was in short supply. The country had never been fitter or healthier.

Fit or not, most civilians were sick of the war. It interfered too much with their lives. It had taken their menfolk away, providing the women, married and unmarried, with all sorts of temptations (if the supply of food went down, the number of unwedded pregnan-cies went up). It also stuck them in jobs they didn't like, making them work very long hours. Meanwhile, there was nothing but bad news from the front. After Dunkirk, the British Army was defeated in Greece, Crete, North Africa, Hong Kong, Singapore; the list of retreats and lost battles seemed never-ending. In the third year of war there seemed to be little hope on the horizon. Why keep up the one-sided fight?

The bluff ex-trades union boss Ernie Bevin announced that spring that Britain had more people engaged in the forces and war industry than any of the other combatant nations, including Germany; but even he had to admit that the State was being forced to imprison one worker in 50,000 for absenteeism. The great problem now was not one of manpower, Bevin said, but of management. Could British managers keep their workers working?

In the spring of 1942 the country lost more time to strikes than it had in 1938. Outside Canterbury, soon to fall victim to the Baedeker raiders, over 1,000 miners went on strike at Betteshanger Colliery for more pay. Three of the ring-leaders were sentenced to jail, but the needs of the time forced the authorities to release them; they were feted as heroes at the local welfare club in Deal. That same month 130,000 British soldiers, most of whom were earning half what the miners did, were captured by the Japanese. Thousands of them were sent to build the infamous Burma Railway on a bowl of rice a day. Only one third of them ever returned home.

Fiddling and petty pilfering flourished. At the great Rowntrees chocolate factory in York workers on the night shift slept hidden in the back of the factory and in the morning filled their pockets with Kit-Kat biscuits. At the nearby airfield where shot-up bombers were repaired and refurbished, night-shift workers made rings and necklaces from the perspex intended for the bombers they were working on and sold them.

In Bath they didn't want the evacuees from the big cities; nor did they welcome the Admiralty staff forced on them as paying guests, because their Lordships would not pay more than a guinea a week for board and lodging. "Guinea-pigs" the citizens of Bath called them contemptuously.

There was complacency and lack of direction. A Major Lock, who set up Bath's Civil Defence system, admitted later, "I didn't expect Bath to be blitzed, except for the odd bomb." In York, there were complaints to the City Council about the cost of the coffins they insisted on stocking in case the city was attacked, and it was decided to allow the head of the ARP Service, a Mr Cooke, to be called up for the Army. In Canterbury, especially at weekends, only half of the fire-watchers turned up for duty; and, in spite of the warning of London and Manchester, where whole streets had burned down because shop-owners had locked up their shops at night and taken the keys home with them, the local merchants were still doing exactly that.

Many of these provincial citizens had still not grasped the realities of the total war in which they were engaged. They simply could not learn the lesson of Poland and other Eastern European countries invaded by Hitler, where a policy of deliberate genocide was being carried out. If Hitler won, the British nation would be enslaved, its intellectual classes wiped out, its male citizens transported elsewhere, its females required only for whatever services they might render the conqueror.

Even their leaders lived in a kind of cloud-cuckoo land, cheerfully planning for a post-war future before there was the remotest hope of victory. That spring, the veteran York businessman and sociologist, Seebohm Rowntree, was safely tucked away in his big Georgian house, busy working on a post-war reconstruction plan for the country at the request of the Liberal Party. It was designed to make a happier and better Britain, or at least to provide a party manifesto that would gain the Liberals votes in the first post-war election, if there ever was one.

Privately, the Rowntree family abhorred the conflict. They were Quakers like so many of York's great families. Jealously they guarded the secret that their huge chocolate factory housed a shell-filling plant (a secret not revealed until well after the war) and they were horrified when a scion of the family actually had the temerity to volunteer for service with the local Home Guard and wear uniform in public!

In Canterbury, another German target to be, the new Archbishop—recently translated from the See of York—Dr William Temple, who affected the old-fashioned clerical gaiters and frock coat of a nineteenth-century divine, still could not bring himself to make a definite statement on the Church of England's attitude to the war. Although many of his young chaplains now languished in German, Italian or Japanese prison camps or were dead on the field of battle, he still felt that although the war was a *righteous* one, it was not a *holy* one. It would be wrong for the nation to range itself against its fellow Christians in Germany. Vicars who sided with Dr Temple were careful, when praying that our aircraft might return from their operations, to add significantly, *"if it be Thy will"*. Soon the good Doctor would find himself sitting on the steps of his cathedral in the middle of the night wondering what had happened.

This lack of understanding about the realities of war was fed by an active left-wing element, who were not involved personally in the war but who felt they had every right to censure those who were. People such as Aneurin Bevan, who could not or would not fight even though they were young enough for the Services, were skilled in criticizing the conduct of the war in Parliament and in the Press. Churchill called Bevan "a squalid nuisance"; while his bullying tactics, flushed face, wild forelock and high-pitched Welsh voice made little impact on the Commons, he did influence the public when his speeches were reported in such popular papers as the *Daily Herald* and *Daily Mirror*.

The *Mirror* was particularly effective in the provinces, where it appealed to the working class, now being fostered by full employment in the war industry, where wages were rocketing. It attracted its readers with a nice mix of pin-ups and sustained campaigns against "Colonel Blimps" and "Army bullshit". Cassandra, the former copy-writer William Connor, used his typewriter like a machine gun to attack "the war at the top" which was being run, he said, by "an expert in reactionary party management" and by "a junta of elderly men who have been bred like racehorses to behave in accordance with the stud book".[1] Even as British servicemen lay dying on battlefields on three continents and victory seemed an impossible dream, Cassandra was taking it upon himself to issue, on behalf of the nation, a demand for better conditions after the war:

> They [the people] want a parliament representative of the people and not a legislature devoted to the interests of property. . . . They want homes and cities planned for the health and happiness of the community and not the enrichment of speculators, smart businessmen and absentee landlords.[2]

By March, 1942, even Morrison, the First World War conscientious objector and long-serving Labour MP who was now Home Secretary, had had enough. He warned the *Mirror* bosses that if they did not want to suffer the fate of the *Daily Worker*, the Communist paper which had been closed down, they had better change their editorial policy. A few days later Cassandra joined the Army.

Thus, at this nadir of the Second World War for Britain, they played their little games, oblivious to the realities of the conflict, seemingly unaware of the fact that the nation was fighting for survival. For if Britain were defeated by Nazi Germany, as SS General Walter Darré, the Reich's "racial expert", had already declared:

> We shall make an end of Englishmen. Able-bodied men will be exported as slaves to the Continent. The old and the weak will be exterminated. All men remaining in Britain as slaves will be sterilized.[3]

There were, however, a few realists who were forced by circumstances or duty to take the German threat from the air seriously, although there had not been a heavy raid on Britain since the invasion of Russia the previous June. Now that these new tip-and-run raiders were sneaking in with ever-increasing frequency by night as well as day, the night-fighter pilot was at last coming into his own.

For nearly three years night-fighters had been a much neglected arm of the Royal Air Force, with all the glory going to the "day boys" who had won the Battle of Britain in 1940. Their aircraft had been mostly obsolete, or converted day-fighters, and their equipment for finding an enemy intruder had been minimal—mainly "carrots and more carrots", as one cynical night-fighter pilot had summed up the pre-1941 situation.

In fact, the hoary old tale about carrots was a cover for the first experiments conducted by the RAF with airborne radar, or as it was still called A-I interception.[4] One budding night-fighter navigator, Jimmy Rawnsley, known on account of his small stature as "the Little Man", described his first encounter with the top-secret device at a lecture given by a civilian behind locked doors at his base at Middle Wallop.

> A-I, the boffin said, works on the same principle as an ordinary sound echo. You shout "boo" across a valley and, after a short interval, the echo shouts "boo" back at you. You time the interval and knowing the speed of sound you can work out the distance across the valley. . . . Now if you use some sort of directional ear trumpet like a sound detector you can tell the direction from which the "boo" is coming.[5]

The boffin went on:

> All the A-I does is to send out a series of radio "boos". If there is another aircraft within range, an echo bounces back from it and the A-I tells you the range and the bearing.[6]

It all sounded very simple. In practice it was not. The A-I set, mounted in the observer's position, consisted of two cathode tubes which gave off a series of green blips that represented the boffin's "boos". By juggling these blips, the operator could, if he were lucky and talented, interpret the position and movement of the target, the details of which he then fed to the pilot so that he could go in for the kill.

But even if the observer was lucky and talented, the A-I set was unreliable and did not prove as efficient as its makers claimed. Its range was limited. All too often the blip disappeared at crucial moments. Some unskilled operators even continued the chase after the enemy plane had long disappeared off the scope. In the end the Command had to carry out a purge of unreliable operators—Rawnsley himself described it as a witch-hunt.

This, then, was the weapon—a Beaufighter fitted with an A-I set—with which the British were going to fight the aerial battle for those many cities which were not protected by General Pile's guns.

But over the winter of 1941/42 the German boffins had been equally busy. Back in September, 1940, the Germans had introduced the idea of a pathfinder force, a group of expert pilots who would light up the target for the more inexperienced crews to follow. By 1941 this special force, KG 100, or "fire-lighters" as their RAF opponents called them, were flying into the attack using radio beams.

Naturally, from prisoners and shot-down German aircraft, the RAF experts soon learnt of this new development and set about countering the enemy radio beams, reading them and deflecting them. But, as soon as the British did so, the Germans simply changed to another beam. As the months passed the German and British boffins fought a secret war, trying to outguess and outwit each other.

The prime mover on the British side in this battle of the airwaves was the Scottish son of a Guards sergeant, thirty-year-old Dr R. V. Jones, a member of Scientific Intelligence, an offshoot of the SIS. A practical joker of some repute, who was not afraid of treading on toes—that was why he was never honoured for his contributions to victory—he had been fighting the enemy in this field since 1940.

Already the young Oxford scientist had guessed that the Germans, who had been dormant all winter and spring, were planning something new. For a while their operators had been sending spoof messages to make the British think that they were coming, while they had quietly been moving their squadrons down from Holland to Western France for the real thing. Jones had seen through that particular trick; he had even wagered that "there would be so many clues obtainable from the prior engagements for a genuine move back of the bomber force that I offered to give six weeks' notice of any major new bombing threat to England".[7]

In late March Jones had given that warning, pointing out that the Germans were going to use a new frequency for their direction beams. He also guessed that they would leave "the old modulation frequency on the transmission, so that we could continue to hear and jam it, but [would superimpose] a supersonic frequency above the limit of human hearing".[8]

Shortly thereafter, the jamming unit Wing 80 had added a supersonic modulation to their jammers. But Jones insisted this new frequency should not be used until the enemy started to use the supersonic beams; he did not want to warn the Germans that he had outguessed them.

However, on the evening of 23 April, 1942, as the German attack force started to warm up on their fields in France, the RAF jammers failed to detect anything. Soon fifty percent of the German bombers were reaching their targets; normally, when jamming was successful, the average was about thirteen per cent. Later, the official enquiry would show that the jamming sets contained a basic design fault. As Jones remarked in disgust, "Once again an elementary mistake which should never have been made had cost many lives. This time I was so sickened that I did not even say that someone should be shot."[9]

They came in fast and low, sweeping across the Channel at wave-top height to dodge the coastal radar. At nearly 300mph, the twenty-five German bombers flashed over the coast of south-west England. The novelist John Fowles, then a teenager, who had already seen the night sky burn bright red to the west over Plymouth when it was blitzed the previous year, caught a glimpse of one of them, "camouflaged dark green and black, blue-bellied, Balkan-crossed, slim, enormous, a two-engined Heinkel, real, the war real, terror and fascination, pigeons breaking from the beeches in a panic".[10] Then it was gone, heading for some still unsuspecting target.

High above the startled youth, the men of the 307th Polish Squadron, whose task it was to defend this sector of the Home Front, milled around impotently in the night sky, cursing the Germans, cursing their radar, cursing every damn thing. For not only had the German Director of Operations introduced directional signals via supersonic frequencies this night, but his boffins had also begun to jam the radar. The Polish operators, locked in the darkness of their compartments, were faced with a confusing mess of swaying blips and dots on their A-I screens which made no sense whatsoever. They were, in short, fighting blind.

Unopposed, the German bombers raced in for the kill, speeding over the peaceful countryside below as one observer post after another took up their flight, frantically calling HQ to give the enemy planes' latest position. Elsewhere, in their concrete underground chambers with blue-uniformed WAAFs clambering up and down ladders in front of the glowing area maps with their counters, anxious controllers tried to guess where the Jerries might attack that night.

In Exeter the sirens sounded their warning. For three years the city had lived in a fool's paradise. The volunteers who manned the Civil Defence had even been shy of wearing their navy-blue battle-dress for fear of being ridiculed by their fellow citizens. The locals mocked them as "part-time darts players". Indeed, the local authorities felt it was the task of the newly-formed National Fire Service[11] to look after the city's safety; after all, the State wasn't paying these healthy young men, who were probably dodging the Forces' call-up anyway, just to laze about their stations playing cards, drinking endless mugs of tea and polishing the engines' brass. To protect the city's most important cultural target from fire, there were exactly fifteen volunteers (St Paul's had several score), mostly women drawn from a group called "The Lovers of the Cathedral". As it happened, the Cathedral was not hit—not, at least, during the first Baedeker raid . . .

This night, when the real war started for Exeter, the bombers did not need the towers of Exeter's Cathedral to guide them to their objectives. The rays which British inefficiency had failed to jam did that for them. Almost as soon as the first large flares—"Christmas trees", as the German pilots called them—came sailing down, bathing all below in a glowing, unnatural light, the leading wave of bombers came swooping in.

They were confident that nothing could stop them. They knew from previous aerial reconnaissance that the city below was defenceless. Pile had had no guns to spare for this militarily unimportant target. As for the Tommy night-fighters, the German pilots reckoned they would be able to carry out their mission and be speeding back home for the usual champagne and thick pea soup before the former located them.

Their target was the area around the Cathedral. It was easily identified. Swooping low, they were dropping their mixed load of fire-bombs and high explosive almost before the sirens had ceased. "Exeter is a jewel," they had been told at their evening briefing. Now they set about deliberately wrecking that jewel. Lübeck and Rostock had to be avenged.

Round and round they circled over the Cathedral, that masterpiece of creative imagination with the longest uninterrupted vaulting in the world, dropping their bombs and coming down as low as 250 feet to machine-gun the harassed rescue workers. Some of the team leaders, who wore white tin helmets for identification, threw the helmets away because they thought the German gunners were deliberately aiming at them. The heart of Exeter was being consumed by a sea of flame, as somewhere up above the Poles sought the attackers in vain.

But the Poles were not the only ones chasing the German bombers that night, as the flickering glow lit up the sky over Exeter, visible from over thirty miles away. Fighter ace John Cunningham and his observer Jimmy Rawnsley were flying a routine night patrol in their Beaufighter when their controller informed them of the attack on Exeter. Although Exeter was in the sector being defended by the Poles, they asked for and received permission to "poach".

Cunningham, who had already won the DSO and DFC in aerial combat, gave the night-fighter full throttle and raced to the defence while Rawnsley crouched over his green-glowing radar set, trying to spot one of the attackers. But it was Cunningham who was first to shout, "I believe I can see it!"

The skipper was right; there it was! Now, as Rawnsley recalled after the war, "We were so close that the blip hovered on the brink of disappearing. And then suddenly it seemed to split into two, and one part rushed away from us."[12]

"*Dive!*" he shrieked over the intercom. "He's diving away!"

Cunningham rammed the Beaufighter's nose down. But the contact was dropping away at an incredible speed. Rawnsley had never seen anything move so fast on his screen before. Had the Jerries brought out a new fighter with remarkable extra acceleration? Then he noticed that "the other half of the blip was also receding, but it was well above us". Suddenly he realized his mistake. He was "trying to intercept the bombs that had just been dropped by the raider"—not the actual bomber![13] Hence the tremendous burst of speed.

Hastily Rawnsley gave fresh instructions to his pilot. But it was already too late. By the time Cunningham had flattened out and had

38

begun to climb to the attack once more, their "customer", as they called the intruder, was on his way home.

By now all the German bombers were racing back across the Channel in triumph. Without the loss of a single plane they had set a great deal of central Exeter on fire, whole terraces of splendid eighteenth-century houses—Dix's Field, Bedford Circus, the upper part of Southernhay West—some of which were considered the finest in the country outside of Bath. Only the Cathedral itself remained miraculously undamaged.

They also left behind them some sixty or seventy people dead and perhaps twice that number seriously injured.[14] The still smouldering city was buzzing with all sorts of rumours, some tragic, some bizarre: the young mother, arteries severed by flying glass, who had bled to death before she could reach the hospital; the ARP warden blown off his bike and thrown head-first into a sewage pond; the man blasted from his bed and hurled across the street, right through a closed window, to land in a strange room where an old and very deaf woman slept on, totally unaware of what was happening all about her!

There was bewilderment too. Why Exeter, the citizens asked? There were no military targets for the enemy to destroy, no war industry, no munitions factories, no barracks, nothing. Why had they attacked them? Some people reasoned, perhaps correctly, that the Germans had come to destroy the Cathedral. Since the war the Dean had ordered the twin towers of the Cathedral closed to visitors. The only people allowed up the narrow winding stairs to the top of the towers were the fire-watchers. What assurance did the citizens have that this handful of middle-aged men and women could put out any German incendiary which landed up there? The place could turn into a blazing inferno in a matter of minutes, guiding the German attackers straight towards Exeter. As diarist James Lansdale Hodson noted, many people felt that "the Cathedral ought to be dynamited because it was a guide and target for the bombers".[15] Why not blow it up and have done with it? Then the Germans wouldn't return to Exeter. In April, 1942, "our great cultural heritage", as the relieved Dean called his undamaged Cathedral, seemingly meant little to the ordinary man and woman in Exeter.

As the German bombers were landing on their French airfields, other bombers—British this time—were returning to their fields in eastern England. They, too, had had "a wizard trip" and had "pranged" their target well and truly. They richly deserved their breakfast of bacon and eggs, for they had plastered their target, Rostock, for a second time.

"Tremendous damage is reported," Goebbels noted that morning. "All long-distance communication has been interrupted. . . . Seventy per cent of all houses in the centre of Rostock are said to have been destroyed." As a result, "the Führer is in an extremely bad humour", and so, Goebbels went on:

> I consider it absolutely essential that we continue with our rigorous reprisal raids. . . . Like the English we must attack centres of culture, especially those which have only little anti-aircraft guns.[16]

Carried away by anger at this new raid on Rostock, the Germans, normally so skilled at propaganda, made a major blunder in the war of words that was to accompany the new campaign. The German Foreign Office, run by ex-champagne salesman Joachim von Ribbentrop—who, as ambassador to the Court of St James before the war, had shocked King George by saluting him with the Nazi "Heil Hitler" greeting—decided it was up to him to explain what the Luftwaffe was doing over England.

We do not know who the backroom boy was who dreamed up the idea, but whoever it was, he somehow came across Karl Baedeker, the German publisher born in 1801 who invented the modern travel book. In his thirties, the bearded, bespectacled German traveller came to England and toured the country before compiling his guide-book, with its characteristic shorthand: "*Exeter, commercial city in SW England, Anglican bishop's seat, walled old town, Norman-Gothic cathedral . . .*" etc, etc. And for each of the medieval English cities that he visited, from York to Canterbury, he gave his sign of approval in the form of three stars.

Thus it was that at the 12.30 press conference at the German Foreign Ministry in Berlin the following day, 24 April, the Ministry's spokesman, a suitably blue-blooded aristocrat, Baron Gustav Braun von Sturm, announced that in reprisal for the bombing of Lübeck and Rostock, "We shall go all out to bomb every building in Britain marked with three stars in the Baedeker Guide."[17]

This was a major propaganda error; soon everyone in Berlin was blaming someone else, including Hitler, for having divulged the plan. But the damage was done; the Germans had revealed their intentions quite clearly. The Baedeker raids had begun and the war had entered a new and merciless stage.

FOUR

Saturday 25 April, 1942.
Over South-West England it was a fine, bright day. The Forces weather forecasters[1] predicted it would be a near perfect night, too, with clear visibility and a "bombers' moon". Not that this would have worried the citizens of Bath unduly. The Georgian city had had alerts enough over the last three years, but they virtually all proved false alarms. Being in the flight-path of Luftwaffe formations heading for the nearby port of Bristol, Bath was used to German bombers passing overhead. In two and a half years the city had suffered less than twenty casualties.

So the people went about their weekend shopping and prepared for a night in the pubs, or more likely in front of the fire, listening to the BBC and that weekend treat, "Saturday Night Theatre".

On the other side of the Channel there was some cloud and a little rain, but that did not deter the Luftwaffe ground crews in their black overalls, as they busied themselves with the parked Heinkels and Dorniers. That very afternoon the Führer had announced to the *Reichstag*:

> Should the idea of continuing air warfare against the civilian population prevail in England, I should like to make the following declaration before all the world: I shall find myself compelled in the future to make a reply which will bring great grief to the British—"*I shall give blow for blow!*"[2]

This was to be a major attack, with 163 bombers employed. They were scraping the barrel, with over a third of crews coming from reserve training units, but the "greenbeaks" were in good spirit, eager to start their first mission. The ground crews were eager too.

41

They wanted to finish their tasks, get cleaned up, and change into their number one uniform. For this was Saturday night and there were good times to be had in the surrounding towns. Many of them had long-standing relationships with obliging French girls—already there had been 100,000 illegitimate children born in France with German fathers—and for those without a girlfriend there were Army brothels enough, carefully supervised by Wehrmacht doctors and segregrated into those for officers and those for other ranks. There was food aplenty too and the *Zivilisten* were friendly. Hadn't the Germans brought full employment to Occupied France for the first time since the early '20s? Even an ordinary airman could "live like God in France" these days.[3]

But among the several hundred excited aircrew and mechanics there was one man who, in spite of his uniform, was strangely out of place, perhaps even a little apprehensive about what was to come, though he dared not show it. His name was Guenther Hoenicke, a former newspaperman in his late twenties, who now belonged to one of Goebbels's "Propaganda Companies", a hundred or so reporters and photo-journalists organized on military lines with a regular officer in command, who went into action with the forward troops in order to achieve that immediacy of battle beloved by the Ministry of Propaganda and People's Enlightenment.

Hoenicke had never flown on a bombing mission against England before. Although his pilot had assured him that their target for tonight lacked virtually all military importance and was, therefore, not defended, he was worried. He had heard from comrades in the *Propagandakompanie* about the intense flak they had encountered when they had flown on raids against London and the like. But he swallowed his fears, smiled much too often and found himself going to urinate every few minutes, a sure sign of nerves. If only that fool over there would stop whistling "*Wir Fahren gegen Enge-land, ahoi!*"

Soon the pilots and crews in their fur jackets, parachutes over their shoulders, fumbling with their maps, were beginning to move to the door. Outside engine after engine burst into life, filling the evening air with the stink of petrol. Little tractors drawing lines of empty wagons which had contained bombs were rumbling back to the stores. Ground crew men were wiping their greasy hands on cotton waste and, despite regulations prohibiting smoking, taking half-smoked "lung torpedoes" from behind their ears and lighting up. There was no time for nerves now. The process had caught Hoenicke up in its machinery. He had to go.

42

Minutes later the first green start flares were whooshing into the sky and over at the control tower the signal lamps were flashing on and off. The pilots opened their throttles. The bombers started to rumble down the tarmac. The great force was under way. The largest attack on Britain since Hitler had invaded Russia in June, 1941, was being launched, its objective Bath.

Like all the rest of the cathedral cities to be bombed by the Germans in the Baedeker campaign, Bath had had a good war so far. Bomb damage and casualties were so rare that when bombs *were* dropped on the city on Good Friday, 1941, morbid curiosity-seekers actually sneaked into the crypt of St James's Church, where eight bodies were left unattended, to view the dead. Shortly thereafter, seven of the bodies were removed. But due to some oversight one body was left behind, without a coffin, for a week; it was only when the stench penetrated to the congregation in the church above that the eighth body was finally disposed of.

But if the average citizen of Bath was unprepared for what was to come, members of the city's fire brigades were all too aware of what they might face. By 1942 the local National Fire Service men were hardened veterans of all the big raids on Bristol. They had also fought blazes caused by German bombs as far away as Swansea and Birmingham, towing their pumps behind old taxis for want of better vehicles. There was also armed help available locally in the form of the 87th and 125th Night-fighter Squadrons based at Colerne and Charmy Down respectively—though in the event their part in what happened was hardly efficacious. Of the two hundred-odd German, British and Polish planes engaged over Bath this night, the only two to be lost were British. In the midst of the attack one unfortunate pilot, Pilot Officer McNair, ran out of fuel. As he desperately tried to restart the engine of his Hurricane, a German latched on to him. There was nothing McNair could do but bail out. He landed safely, if bruised, to face a monstrous rocket from his C.O. the following morning. It was the only funny thing to happen over Bath that night.

At a quarter past ten the first stream of bombers crossed the coast on a broad front between Devon and the Isle of Wight. As Guenther Hoenicke recorded with typical German *schadenfreude*, "The Tommies don't yet know where the bombers are heading. They feel secure."[4] Down below anxious RAF radar operators hunched over the dials of their sets trying to assess what the German target could be. Were they heading for Bristol, they wondered, as the Germans flew on over Hampshire and Wiltshire.

Over Salisbury the "fire-lighters" of the German 123th Reconnaissance Group started to drop their Christmas-tree flares to guide the oncoming bombers, leaving behind them a lane of sinister icy-white beacons. On the ground, sirens began to track their progress with their chill wail.

At one minute to eleven exactly the Red Alert, meaning "raiders imminent", was flashed to Bath. The local controller ordered the sirens sounded, as over Bristol the AA guns began to thunder, for the controller still thought the German armada was heading for the port.

In Bath firemen began to tumble from their bunks. The Civil Defence workers, for their part, took their time. Many of them had had a few pints that night and it was probably yet another false alarm. Leading Fireman Tom Gale, who was off duty at home that night, began dressing hastily to return to his station. Then the windows began to rattle. He reassured his wife that it was only the wind, but the veteran of many a blitz on Bristol knew differently. It was the real thing this time. He hurried outside.

ARP worker Ron Shearn was another who thought it was a false alarm until he went outside. He spotted the sinister, glittering flare hanging over the city centre and gasped as he saw a dark shape swoop out of the sky, black eggs tumbling from its belly. This time the Luftwaffe's target really was Bath!

High above the city, now outlined a stark white against the blackness of the night, Guenther Hoenicke made his notes for the morning edition of the Führer's own newspaper, the *Völkischer Beobachter:*

> *Now!* The first flare bombs from our leaders light up the land like day. Beneath, the River Avon winds through the countryside like a silver thread. Here below us is the great loop in the middle of which the town lies. And now the first small incendiaries go down.[5]

On the morrow, under the headline, "*Annihilating Reprisal Attack on the English Town of Bath: Lübeck and Rostock Avenged!*", Hoenicke would detail what happened next. It was a typical piece of National Socialist prose, full of bombast and Wagnerian undertones, clipped harsh sentences to suggest violent action, replete with exclamation marks to make sure that even the most stupid reader could not fail to see the emphasis.

Suddenly in front of us there is a great towering glare, which dazzles us even in the cockpit with its flaming red! A huge cloud bursts up from below, sinisterly lit by the greedy self-devouring flames. A gas holder has exploded in the gas works!

In a second the fire spreads and casts a flaming light over the city. We go down still lower. Beneath us we see rows of burning houses. Smoke rises from them and thickens into a black cloud which lies over the town in a threatening pall. We recognize the streets as well. Fire and destruction are raging in them! Our commander searches calmly for a new target. We fly over it.

"Bomb doors open. *Let go!*"

Heavy bombs fall. Then waiting—a strained pause. Once again there is a flash below and where all had been dark before there is a sudden light, an unpleasant light for the English. *Annihilation!*

The bombs have exploded and met their target. Fresh formations are coming up behind and new explosions continually occur. One wave after another visits this town with death and destruction.[6]

But it was not all so exact and planned as the airborne reporter recorded. The inexperienced German pilots were losing their way all over South-West England and dropping their bombs at random. Chippenham was hit, as were Trowbridge, Keynsham and Bradford-on-Avon. But how could even a novice pilot mistake Dorchester or Stroud, which were both bombed, for Bath? Some even ranged as far as South Wales.

One of these strays, a Junkers 88, had become lost almost as soon as it crossed the English coast. After some time it was reported in the Hereford area where a Beaufighter, on a training mission to test its A-I radar, jumped it. The pilot of the Beaufighter, Pilot Officer Wyvill, was all set to shoot the lost plane down when it took violent evasive action. For a few moments Wyvill lost visual contact, but his A-I set was functioning well, and the German plane still showed as a green blip on the operator's tiny screen. Taking his directions from the operator, Wyvill rapidly found the German again. As the unsuspecting Junkers levelled out, Wyvill came to within fifty yards, finger poised over the firing button. The bomber seemed to fill the horizon and this time Wyvill knew he couldn't miss. He pressed the button. The Beaufighter's cannon chattered into activity. Huge lumps of metal broke away from the Junkers' fuselage and blue flames streamed upwards from the shattered starboard engine.

There was a sudden flash of white as a parachute burst open. It was the radio operator, already wounded, making his escape. The observer followed him a moment later. But the pilot and the rear gunner remained strapped into their seats as the crippled German plane went into its final dive, straight into the mountain below.

Even if there were many strays that night during the first raid on Bath, plenty of German bombers *did* reach their target. Wave after wave of them filled the sky as the bombs fell on the practically defenceless town. They zoomed in low and machine-gunned anyone foolish enough to be out on the streets, which were now as bright as day. A warden running home to alert his wife to the danger found her dead, crumpled on the cobbles. She had been riddled by bullets as she ran to the shelter. Ambulances were shot up as their women drivers raced to St Martin's Hospital, where a Czech refugee doctor by the name of Fritz Koehn ran the medical team. By the time Bath's two-day blitz was over, the Koehn team alone had dealt with some 200 wounded.

One terrified little girl, only eight years old, had to urge her mother and grandmother out of the house. Both of them deaf and blind, they were forced to rely on the child to alert them to danger. Forty years later she remembers:

> It was like daylight outside. The sky seemed alight. It would suddenly light up with bright sheets of light. You could see the aircraft come over. They were machine-gunning as they came over Twerton Roundhill. You could see the red tracer bullets flying. I looked up and saw a plane machine-gunning along the back of the allotments. It seemed to confront us. The aircraft was glass-fronted and a face was visible. It was really pale in the light.[7]

The little girl was not the only one to see a German that night. Fireman Tom Gale did, too. He had been trying to rescue some trapped people in Lower Bristol Road when he looked up and saw a bomb whistling down from the dark shape of a German plane. He threw himself to the ground, but the blast of the detonation sucked the air from his lungs. Choking and gasping for breath, he lapsed into unconsciousness. He awoke to find a frantic police sergeant slapping his face and crying wildly, "Wake up! Wake up! *Everything's on fire!*"

Somehow he staggered to his feet. He and the policeman were the only ones alive in that street. Twenty-eight houses had been destroyed by the bomb and all their inhabitants had been killed.

The casualties and damage were mounting steadily. Amid the first signs of panic, however, there were also moments of black comedy. Assuming that the bombs dropping on Bath were really part of a bigger raid on Bristol, one fire squad set off for the port, a fireman in the party actually passing his own house as it went up in flames. It was only when they reached Bristol that they were told they had come to the wrong town; the raid was on their home town.

But if the regulars fought both the confusion and the incipient panic in some places, such as the big Scala public shelter, the volunteers and pressed men of the local Civil Defence were not standing up to the attack so well. Many of them fled to the shelters, leaving the numerous small fires to burn themselves out; and one top-secret government report of the time, not released till thirty years later, pointed out that it was only the action of the NFS which prevented "serious conflagrations", since fire prevention "was seriously disorganized".

With a strong east wind blowing, the fires spread rapidly. Added to the failure of the water mains and the disappearance of the firewatchers to the shelters, this meant that the city was in serious danger of being burned down. As the same report noted, "Heavy attack on the town centre might well have caused its complete destruction."[8]

Finally, after nearly three hours of uninterrupted bombing, the sirens started to sound the All Clear. Grateful survivors began to stagger from the Anderson and Morrison shelters—like Eric Davies, who had dug his own shelter in his back garden—to discover that "the Gasworks were already burning. That was the biggest conflagration, but there were fires everywhere."[9] The whole horizon was one stretch of lurid orange flame, against which the shattered buildings of central Bath were silhouetted a stark black. It was a perfect target for the second attack.

While the crews were debriefed, drinking real bean coffee instead of the usual ersatz, here and there allowing themselves a cognac or a stiff shot of neat gin, their favourite "clear one", as they called it, the ground crews worked feverishly to re-arm the planes while petrol bowsers went up and down the line pumping fuel into empty tanks.

Tired but triumphant, Guenther Hoenicke tapped away at his portable typewriter, preparing his article for the Monday papers.

"In the idyllic hotels and summer houses of Bath," he wrote, apparently imagining Bath to be like a German spa, "high British staffs of British defensive forces have taken up their headquarters. Here they have been working out the criminal plans which have led to the destruction of irreplaceable works of culture in our trading towns of Lübeck and Rostock and to the terrorization of old German towns." As a result, he boasted,

> German bombers have now brought home to the instigators of these attacks the effect of German bombs on their own houses with powerful reprisal attacks, and thereby have not only hit many of the parties responsible for such warfare, but at the same time given them the proof that Germany is not inclined to look on inactively at their crazy ideas of our destruction.
>
> By order of the High Command of the Wehrmacht, strong formations of German aircraft carried out a heavy reprisal raid on Bath . . . Even lively interference could not prevent the German planes from reaching their target. . . . Countless incendiaries were dropped and then blazing fires broke out, especially in the centre. The attack, which went entirely to plan, repaid the British for their wanton destruction of living quarters, cultural monuments and welfare arrangements in ancient German cities.[10]

Although Hoenicke referred to military targets at Bath, however confused he was about the Admiralty HQ located there, statements made by Luftwaffe prisoners and documents which subsequently fell into British hands make it quite clear that this was purely and simply a reprisal raid. In a speech made by *Hauptmann* Otto Brechtle at the time, the text of which was later captured, the message is unequivocal: "Using the tactics so successfully employed by the enemy against Lübeck and Rostock, concentrated raids of short duration were carried out for the first time to minimize defensive action. . . . The raid on Bath had a really annihilating effect."[11] A few days later Goebbels wrote in his diary, "London now admits that intense damage has been done in Bath. . . . There is talk of scenes like those at Coventry. That's the sort of music we like to hear!"[12]

Neither the attackers nor the victims were concerned with the ethics of the matter that night, as forty more bombers prepared to deal Bath another blow. In Bath itself, while rescue workers were desperately trying to free people trapped in the flaming ruins, Civil Defence workers were facing another problem—a new kind of delayed action high explosive bomb, which the Germans had dropped all over the city centre. This bomb, equipped with a short fuse, was now beginning to explode—with disastrous effects. Due to the terraced construction of those splendid Georgian houses, whole rows of buildings had collapsed like a stack of cards, trapping hundreds of people in the rubble.

Thousands of survivors were leaving the blazing city, heading for the relative safety of the surrounding countryside—among them, many an evacuee who had fled the capital the year before to escape the London blitz. Many of them made for the caves at Bathampton or the open fields around Padleigh, Wellow, Lansdown and the like. In Lansdown Road there are still residents who remember their parents handing out shoes to the barefoot "trekkers", as they were called, fleeing from their ruined homes, carrying with them the few possessions that they had been able to rescue.

One who stayed behind was Ron Shearn, the ARP man. He had been detailed to stand guard over a pile of dead bodies, stacked like logs, while crowds of bewildered refugees streamed past him down the shattered Lower Bristol Road. Suddenly in the flickering light of a fire nearby, it seemed that one of the bodies moved. Shearn took another more careful look. The body of a three-year-old girl really was moving. He summoned a passing ambulance driver. The latter wasn't convinced. "Better look after the living, chum," he told Shearn. But the ARP man persisted and in the end the driver took the girl to hospital. There she made a complete recovery. Today, somewhere in that part of the world there is a middle-aged housewife, probably with children of her own, who has been granted a whole lifetime by an old man she has never seen.

Others were not so fortunate. Later Shearn and a colleague, Harry Boone, who had only one arm, began tunnelling with the aid of four men of the Home Guard into the wreckage of a house, where a family was reported buried alive. But when the rescuers finally found them all five of the family were dead. One of them, a little girl called Cherry, was found curled in the arms of her father, an RAF man who had come on leave the previous day. But his protective gesture had been in vain. Old and young alike, they had all been killed by the bombs.

At exactly four o'clock on Sunday morning, while rescue workers were still trying to free the trapped and douse the fires, the German bombers came again, catching the hard-pressed city completely by surprise.

William Smith, an ambulance driver, was just loading a dead man into his boxlike vehicle, helped by a pale-faced sixteen-year-old messenger boy, "when Jerry decided to drop a bomb into the river. It threw a great deal of muck out: dead fish, bicycles, bedsteads, etc. We shot under the ambulance to take cover from the muck rather than the bomb."[13]

Albert Davis, a rescue party leader, was in the process of being machine-gunned. "I fell into the gutter and put some paper over my head to protect myself against the machine-gunning. It was stupid, but I did have my white hat on and white hats were a target."[14]

Naturally, the German gunners could not see individual targets and no casualties were reported from machine-gunning that night, but the bullets deterred people from moving about on the streets and helped the new fires to get a real start. Some brave individuals did venture out, however, including Marjorie Horsell, a first-aider. In spite of the bombs, the bullets, the shrapnel cutting the air, she tried desperately to reach her post. But as she reached Upper Bristol Road, she was stopped by a police inspector who told her that the road and the nearby gasworks were a sea of flames; she could go no further. So she took cover. "The German pilots," she recorded later, "were so low that I could see them in the planes and could see the tracer bullets. It was awful to see the faces in the planes."[15]

Later, however, the plucky first-aider did manage to help with the streams of shocked men, women and children who were soon straggling into the aid posts throughout the burning city. There were 1,200 of them in the end. "The casualties, by and large, were usually the less serious: fractured legs, firemen overcome by smoke, shrapnel wounds and grazings. A number were badly shocked and were given hot water bottles and covered with a blanket. Only occasionally was anyone hysterical."[16] A little later Marjorie Horsell nearly became hysterical herself, for when she went to tend an old lady who seemed to have a badly bruised head and attempted "to lift up her hair . . . her scalp came off like a wig!"[17]

As the second raid started to peter out, the authorities began to take stock. The local *Western Daily Press* reporters manfully scribbled away, preparing a highly coloured account of the raid to appear in the Monday edition of the paper, stating that the German bombers were met by "a heavy barrage from the ground defences and RAF fighters took over to engage them. Several dogfights took place over the city and the noise of the crashing bombs mingled with the roar of fighter engines while flares and streams of tracer bullets coloured the moonlit sky."[18] It was all rip-roaring stuff, but not one word of it was true. The Germans had got away with a quite spectacular raid, with the loss of perhaps five aircraft in all, less than three percent of the total raiding force.

Bath's casualty figures, on the other hand, were high. As dawn broke, with twenty fires still burning, first indications were that some fifty people had been seriously injured. Eight houses were known to have either dead or hurt people still trapped beneath them. Roughly 1,400 people were being lodged in various rest centres with thousands more roaming the countryside and surrounding hills. Hundreds of homes, shops and offices had been destroyed. Bath had taken a bad beating—and there was more to come.

So, shocked and apprehensive, the citizens watched in fearful expectation as daylight crept over their shattered city. Some, like Mrs Florence Delve, would never get over what had happened that Saturday night. Already she and her husband had dug out their trapped neighbours; one of them, a little girl named Jean, had died in Mr Delve's arms, although there wasn't a mark on her, save a bruise on her forehead.

The Delves' own home had been destroyed, though they had escaped unhurt. "The first thing I heard was my baby crying," Mrs Delve recalls. "I tried to feed her, but the shock had driven the milk away and I couldn't. I had never smoked till then but I was in such a state that my husband told me to. My teeth were chattering. We never undressed and stayed in the same clothes till Wednesday night. You had to fend for yourself. It had stunned me so I couldn't think for myself. The last time I was safe was when I heard that whistle [of the bombs]. From then on, it was a nightmare that I can only vaguely remember."[19]

But the nightmare was not yet over. There was more death and destruction to come. Bath's suffering had only just begun.

FIVE

General Pile was suffering agonies of doubt that Sunday morning. What were the Germans' intentions in the West Country? First it had been Exeter, now Bath. But was Bath really their primary target? Had they meant to strike Bristol, but been driven off by his AA gunners and forced to jettison their bombs over poor, undefended Bath?

The morning bulletin of the German High Command, preceded by the usual roll of drums and fanfare of trumpets, soon told him that Bath had indeed been the target. The harsh voice of the announcer told the world that Bath had been swamped with thousands of incendiaries and high explosive bombs in an "act of revenge" for the bombing of "cultural monuments" in Germany.

Now Pile had confirmation that the night raid on Exeter was not an isolated incident. The reference to Baedeker and his three stars and now this double attack on Bath were the start of a new bombing campaign against the United Kingdom. The Germans were, as they had indicated themselves, attacking lightly defended or undefended towns of cultural interest. The problem for AA Command, however, was which towns in a country well studded with targets of cultural interest could it defend? General Pile could only stretch his resources so far.

After three years of war, with nearly a quarter of a million British citizens dead or wounded due to enemy air action, Pile still did not have enough anti-aircraft guns to defend the country properly. As he stated himself in a letter to the Chiefs of Staff, he would be forced under present circumstances "to leave 39 scheduled gun-defended areas still undefended and 236 vulnerable points without protection."[1] Now he was being expected to add every cathedral city in the kingdom to his list of places to be defended! Nor had he sufficient mobile batteries or radar sets to be able to switch AA defence from one city to another as the need arose.

But Pile was not in the habit of "bellyaching", as he called it. For three years now he had been making the best of a bad job, fighting the Treasury for money, fighting the apathy of local authorities, the manpower problem, the sheer bloody-mindedness of some brass hats at the War Office. He decided to make the best of what he had. Although he knew it was a retrograde step, he brought his rocket projectors out of retirement. He had moth-balled them back in 1940 during the blitzes on London, for they had little hope of ever hitting a plane. But they might force the enemy attackers up higher, making their aim less certain. And, in view of the public outcry coming from a stricken Bath this Sunday morning, he had to produce guns, whatever their efficiency.

Pile also attempted to acquire more mobile guns, so that he could switch his defences from city to city, but, as he wrote after the war, "It shows what straits we were reduced to when I say that we had to get the War Office to swap the mobile guns at their training camps for some of our static ones—a despairing effort which produced 28 more mobile equipments!"[2]

Pile's next act was to select potential enemy targets for defence. They were Penzance, Truro, Exeter, Bath, Basingstoke, Guildford, Maidstone, Tunbridge Wells, Ashford and Canterbury, with Oxford, Chichester and Brighton added to the list two days later. As if this weren't enough to stretch his slender resources to breaking point, a few days later Pile added Ipswich, Cambridge, Colchester, Chelmsford, Lincoln, Peterborough and York. Not all these places were of great aesthetic value, but Pile reasoned that some of the lesser ones might be attacked by aircraft splitting off from a bigger Baedeker raid.

In the event, Pile got it wrong. Despite the fact that the British had the Ultra decoding system, which gave them almost immediate access to Luftwaffe signals and the code words they used for individual British towns,[3] *and* the fact that the entire German spy network in the country was controlled by MI5, so that it could be used to delude the enemy about targets and damage etc, once again the Germans would outwit the defenders.

Nor had the RAF technicians of No 80 Wing, whose task it was to jam the beams guiding German bombers to their targets, been able to discover what was wrong with their sets. They were, of course, jamming the X-beams on the ordinary modulations, but the harassed operators insisted that the enemy was not using supersonic modulation as Dr Jones had predicted they would; therefore, why switch on their supersonic jammers? In the end Jones forced an enquiry, which discovered that the design of the set was at fault. But that was much later.

So it was that Britain, which ought to have had the most sophisticated air defence system in the whole world—after all, no other country had been so consistently bombed by a first-class air power for nearly two years—went into this new battle of the air inadequately defended, poorly armed with obsolete weapons and employing technical devices on the ground which were patently sub-standard.

It wasn't only General Pile who was experiencing frustration and anger this April Sunday. The RAF Night-Fighter Command had its problems too. For a while now the Germans had been jamming the original A-I airborne radar set, so the RAF had hastily switched to a new model, the Mark Seven set. It was straight from the designers and was suffering from serious teething troubles. If that were not enough, the Mark Seven set was installed in a new Beaufighter with which the crews had had no time to familiarize themselves. As a result, due to the imminence of further German night attacks, the crews were ordered to switch to the Hurricane and Bolton Defiant for this night's flying patrols. But these obsolete pre-war fighters were not equipped with any kind of radar whatsoever. The Beaufighter pilots who took them over dubbed them "cat's-eye fighters" because the crew had to rely exclusively on visual contact, again a retrograde step.

By nightfall that Sunday it had been agreed between the RAF and AA Command that Pile's guns, what there were of them, would be allowed to fire on any raider crossing the coastline. But over Bath and other potential German targets it would be strictly "a fighter night". This meant that no aircraft would be allowed within twenty square miles of the target save the night-fighters. Any other plane would be an enemy. These night-fighters would then cruise at varying heights and covering previously worked-out grids. No anti-aircraft guns would be allowed to fire within this twenty-mile area in case the shells hit their own fighters.

Pile didn't like "fighter nights". The morale of his troops suffered when they were not allowed to fire; and, inevitably, rumours circulated, when no guns opened up, that his crews were asleep on the job. As he later wrote: "Of course, sometimes 'fighter nights' did result in the destruction of a number of German bombers, but at its best it was a chancy business, and at worst it resulted in an enormous lowering of morale of both civilians and troops."[4]

By midnight, with Pile's guns ordered not to shoot, there was a standing patrol of these antiquated Defiants—shot down by the score in France back in 1940—flying over the still smoking city of Bath. Again the British were muddling through. As an embittered and angry Dr Jones stated afterwards, "None of this story is in the *Official History*, which merely records that after 4 May, 'almost everything went wrong for the attackers'."[5]

But before that date arrived many more innocent British men, women and children would have to die.

Just before one o'clock the first of eighty-three German bombers from France started crossing the coast between the Isle of Wight and Torquay. Six minutes later Pile's AA guns opened up at Portland, as the searchlights flicked at the clouds with their icy fingers. To little avail. The intruders sailed on serenely, leaving the brown puffballs of smoke behind them.

A lone Beaufighter pilot, who had been having trouble with his oxygen equipment during the last three hours of his patrol, had just requested permission to return to base when he was told the exciting news that ground radar had picked up "bandits". His tiredness and frustration with the defective apparatus was forgotten in a flash. He opened the throttle and headed towards the coast near Exeter.

At exactly fourteen minutes after one, he made visual contact. There it was, the familiar silhouette of a twin-engined Junkers 88, outlined against the moon which had just risen. It was a perfect target. His "customer" was being presented to him on a silver platter!

The Beaufighter pilot did not hesitate. He closed to within a few hundred yards. The Junkers had apparently not seen him. His thumb pressed down on the firing button. The fighter quivered violently as the shells zipped towards the unsuspecting German. The enemy didn't have a chance. The burst of fire raked the length of the fuselage. The Beaufighter pilot watched his shells striking home, sure he had killed most of the enemy crew with that first burst. The Junkers made an uncontrolled half-roll to port; the attacker veered in the other direction, as the crippled Junkers swung by him only yards away. With smoke streaming from it in a black trail, the Junkers hurtled downwards while the operator tracked its death ride on his radar. A few seconds later the blip disappeared from the little green screen and the operator cheered. The Junkers had gone into the sea off Hope Cove, where its shattered fuselage rests beneath the water to this day.

By now the sirens were beginning to sound again in Bath, and those who had stayed behind braced themselves for yet another attack. The Civil Defence authorities did the same, knowing that on the previous night the fire-watching system had virtually collapsed under the strain. Indeed, the official report on the Saturday night raid stated quite bluntly: "It is the general feeling that the Fire Guard largely disintegrated after the first raid."[6] Now the problem was heightened by the fact that many of the fire-watchers had fled the city with the rest of the trekkers.

Meanwhile the night-fighters were up in force, trying to intercept the intruders before they reached their target, which Control now estimated to be Bath. Wing-Commander Ivins, flying a Hurricane, got in a lucky burst on a Dornier 17. Its right wing was riddled and tracer was seen ripping off pieces of metal from one engine. But just as the jubilant Wing Commander was about to press home his attack, he heard his engine cut out; he had failed to throttle back in his excitement. The Dornier disappeared into some low cloud.

Nearer to Bath, one of the obsolete Defiants tackled a Heinkel, stitching a line of glowing holes along its fuselage. It, too, disappeared and was later claimed as a "probable kill". But still that sinister V formation of the main force kept droning on at a steady 200 miles an hour, heading for the stricken city.

Five minutes later it was the turn of the Germans to attack in the air. A Heinkel came swooping out of the darkness, heading straight for what the inexperienced pilot assumed was a Hurricane. But it was a Defiant, its gun turret located to the rear of the pilot. Perhaps the German crew had never been taught to recognize a Tommy plane which ought to have been phased out of the RAF two years before.

The Defiant's air gunner could hardly believe his eyes. The Heinkel was heading straight into his field of fire! He tensed behind his twin Brownings, watching the black shape of the Heinkel getting larger and larger by the instant. It was a perfect target. Even a gunner with a wooden eye couldn't miss this one. He pressed the firing button. *Nothing happened.*

Fortunately the Heinkel's aim was bad. The German's tracer whizzed harmlessly past the Defiant, which promptly dived for cover while its infuriated gunner cursed his impotent Brownings.

Later he was to discover that, in the flap to prepare the Defiants, someone had not fitted the firing pins.

But a few fighters did manage to intercept the German bomber fleet and rattled some of the young pilots enough to deflect them from the target. One wandered off towards Bristol where it ran into an AA barrage and was thought to have been shot down. A further two ended up bombing Exmouth, while other raiders were reported over Crediton, Bridport and even Cardiff, where the anti-aircraft guns opened up for the first time since the previous spring.

All this meant little to the hard-pressed citizens of Bath, however. For now the great mass of German bombers were zooming in to drop their deadly eggs on the city yet again. Outside the city, those who had fled or lived in the suburbs watched in horror as the flames began to leap higher and higher to the east of Bath.

One of the onlookers was Mrs Florence Delve, still shaken after her terrible experiences the previous night. Her husband was equally rattled. Watching the bombing of the city, Mr Delve was annoyed by an unknown man in uniform who struck a match to light a cigarette. As Mrs Delve recorded many years later, "My husband hit him for six, saying, 'You light another bloody match and I'll hit you to the ground! You call yourself a bloody soldier?' "[7]

Inside the city, however, in spite of the failings of the fire service, the mood was much calmer than on the previous night. At the First Aid posts, there were a few cases of hysteria among the injured and some uncontrolled vomiting was noted; but otherwise the citizens of Bath seemed to be getting accustomed to the mayhem and sudden death.

But the Germans appeared determined to break the spirit of the locals and burn the city down for good. Incendiaries rained down in showers; later it was estimated that four and a half tons had been dropped. Mostly they were the small tube-like fire bombs, which emitted a series of brilliant white sparks before bursting into full flame. If they were tackled immediately, even with the admittedly primitive tools that the fire-watchers possessed—a bag of sand, empty pail or stirrup pump—there was a good chance of putting them out. But once they started to burn, it was damnably difficult to extinguish them.

Soon the water supply began to give out. Few of the amateur fire-watchers, who hated the normally boring night job, knew where the static water tanks were located. So, as the water supply from the river dwindled to almost half the usual level, the fire-watchers ran around in confusion or stood helplessly by as the flames danced through the city. In addition, as more and more buildings collapsed into heaps of rubble and blocked the streets, it became increasingly difficult for the engines and water carts of the National Fire Service to reach the scene of a fire.

One of the worst losses of that second night was Bath's famed Assembly Rooms. After years of neglect the elegant Georgian building had been re-opened in 1939. But an incendiary set fire to the roof and the firemen, rendered impotent by lack of water, could only stand by and watch. Within a short time most of the interior had disappeared, leaving only the Card Room and Club Room intact, plus a decidedly battered sedan chair standing amid the piles of glowing rubble. For some of the more sensitive citizens of Bath this was the most poignant memory of the city's ordeal.

Most, however, were more concerned with survival. The local services broke down and men from the Gloster Regiment were drafted in to help. But the "Diehards" suffered too, as Ron Shearn, the warden, later recalled:

> I'd just got to a horse-trough when I heard a burst of machine-gun fire. I dived for cover near the trough, in the road under the wall. I looked back. Two of them [from the Glosters] were on the ground. One had his head shot off. The second was hit in the leg. . . . The dead man was a lieutenant. I later had a letter from his mother. I told her that her son had died a hero's death—it was better that way.[8]

Many would die alone that night, trapped and screaming for help that would never come, or blown apart so that their remains, looking like offal in a butcher's shop, were later collected in a bucket to be interred in the mass grave at Haycombe Cemetery. Altogether 247 men, women and children were buried at Haycombe, the only sign of their passing today a row of white gravestones.

Some would not believe that their loved ones were dead. One such was Private Eric Davies of the Somerset Light Infantry, who searched endlessly through the rubble of his home in 32 Kingsmead Street, convinced that his wife Millie and their three young children—June, aged five, Pam, aged two, and baby John, six weeks old—could still be in there, buried alive. He haunted the place for a full week, never sleeping, living off sandwiches and cups of tea pressed on him by the good ladies of the WVS, always searching frantically for his missing family, shrugging off any attempt to stop him, ignoring warnings from the local bobbies that he had already been posted as a deserter by his battalion. In the end he found his family. They were all dead. Private Davies walked away without a word. He was never seen again in Kingsmead Street.

A namesake of his, also from the Somersets, also decided that his family was more important to him than the call of duty. After being bombed out with his wife and children, he decided to evacuate them himself.

> I had five shillings to get to near Stroud. We got to Stonehouse and then had no money. We were like gypsies. My wife had some nappies given to her and a coat three times as big as her. We had sixpence left and my wife said I should use it for a pint. The landlord of the pub asked if we were from Bath. I said we were, but were stuck. I wasn't going to beg. He called a man out and said he had a car. The man drove us to Stroud.[9]

But as the Germans began to depart and people like the Davies family fled the shattered city, the ghouls were already emerging from the shadows—looters, looking for easy pickings. As always after a raid, there were a few heartless individuals who would not hesitate to profit from the misfortune of their fellow citizens. As the All Clear started to sound across the burning city, the police posted their signs on wrecked buildings—"*LOOTERS WILL BE SHOT!*"—while others on patrol armed themselves with .38 revolvers, but without ammunition. The Home Guard and helmeted soldiers who patrolled with fixed bayonets did have ammunition, however; moving about in pairs with "one up the spout", they had been ordered to shoot to kill if any looter they apprehended did not stop. There were even gangs of "wide boys" or "spivs" who came from outside, posing as rescue gangs, and systematically looted important buildings, armed with picks and shovels and carrying away their plunder in their own vehicles—fuelled undoubtedly with black-market petrol.

When Private Davies of the Somersets returned to his wrecked house to collect the few possessions that had been salvaged from the ruins, he found they had in the meantime been plundered by an organized gang from London: "My uncle was in a pub and heard them arranging for transport and when the lorry would pick the stuff up."[10]

Davies called the CID who broke into the house where the gang were hoarding the loot they had taken from his place and others. The police even found an East End woman wearing his wife's best dress. But in the end nothing came of it and the woman was acclaimed in the local paper as "a blitz heroine" for having done rescue work. The only compensation Davies ever received for having lost his house and all his possessions was £120 to start a new life. Not that he had much time to ponder the injustice of it all. A year later he was on his way to fight in Sicily and then Italy, slogging his way up the "boot".

Soon after daybreak that Monday morning, the citizens of Bath began to count the cost of their own and the country's complacency and unpreparedness. The WVS and local undertakers started the grim task of piecing bodies together so that they could be identified. In one case a man and a woman were found sitting bolt upright in their chairs three weeks after the raid; both had been gnawed to skeletons by rats. The authorities slowly amassed the casualty figures and assessed damage to property.

As always in small provincial towns, they worked out the details of property damage first. A total of 329 houses and shops had been completely destroyed, with a further 732 having to be demolished. In all, 19,147 buildings had suffered some sort of damage, and two years later only half of them had been repaired. The gutted area of Bath would remain derelict long after the war was over.

The casualties were much harder to assess than the damage to buildings, partly because so many people had left the city after the first raids. But it is generally supposed that 417 men, women and children were killed. Two years after the Baedeker raids, however, in September, 1944, the *Bath and Wilts Chronicle and Herald* reported that 1,272 casualties (including wounded) had resulted from the attacks. This might well have been the true figure—a great blood-letting for a medium-sized city. That Wednesday when MP Rhys Davies stood up in the House of Commons to ask whether the recent attack on Lübeck had been directed at military targets—he'd heard that there had been terrible destruction and loss of civilian life—he was shouted down by enraged fellow MPs with the cry *"What about Bath?"*

Lübeck's most famous son, Thomas Mann, living in exile in California, could find no sympathy for his fellow countrymen now that they were attacking British cultural targets. Speaking on American radio that month he said: "When one realizes what is to come to Germany's cities—of necessity, and justifiably so—then one is overcome by a mild shock. Lübeck and Rostock have been the merest tastes of what is coming. It will be terrible and—I repeat—rightly so."

A day later he wrote, "When I saw a picture of Lübeck I felt rather strange. . . . Forty percent of the Old Town is destroyed, they say. But what matters? Since 1933, the Lübeckers have been the worst kind [of Nazis]."[11]

These were not the kind of sentiments calculated to endear him to the citizens of his former town, even those who were anti-Nazi. But what did it matter that terrible spring? The gloves were off now. The very nature of war was changing. The object was no longer simply to destroy military targets, but to kill and demoralize as many civilians as humanly possible. What the planners on both sides wanted was to cause such misery that the wretched civilians would force their leaders to sue for peace. As a thesis it was quite absurd and the planners should have known it. The German blitz on London and Britain's other great cities back in 1940–41 had shaken the morale of the civilians but had not broken it. The vastly greater bombing of Germany's cities now to come would equally fail to break the morale of the German people.

But it hurt all the same, and strengthened Germany's resolve to pay the Tommies back in their own kind. Rostock was bombed yet again by Harris's men and Goebbels noted in his diary:

> Last night the heaviest air attack yet launched had the seaport of Rostock once again as its objective. Tremendous damage is reported . . . all long distance communication has been interrupted. . . . Seventy per cent of all houses in the centre of Rostock are said to have been destroyed. I now consider it absolutely essential that we continue with our reprisal raids. Like the English we must attack centres of culture, especially those which have only little anti-aircraft guns.[12]

Hitler evidently thought the same, for after lunching with him that day Goebbels described him as "very angry about the latest English attack on Rostock".

> But he also gave me a few figures about our attack. . . . The Führer declared that he would repeat these raids night after night until the English were sick and tired of terror attacks. He shares my opinion absolutely that cultural centres, health resorts and civilian centres must be attacked now. . . . There is no other way of bringing the English to their senses. They belong to a class of human beings with whom you can talk only after you have first knocked out their teeth![13]

Soon the local *gauleiter* would be reporting to Goebbels that "seven-tenths of the city have been wiped out. More than 100,000 people had to be evacuated. . . . There was, in fact, panic."[14] By now Goebbels knew that the raids on the English Baedeker cities must continue. If the Tommies could panic German civilians, then the Luftwaffe had to step up its efforts to do the same to English civilians.

Such considerations did not deter Harris and his planners at their headquarters in High Wycombe. Indeed, the fact that British cities, for the most part undefended, were being bombed as a direct result of their attacks on Germany never worried Harris. Right from the start of the war he had made it quite clear that he saw "only one possible way of bringing pressure to bear on the Boche and certainly only one way of defeating him; that was by air bombardment".[15]

Just after taking over as head of Bomber Command Harris had made his point again. "There are a lot of people who say that bombing cannot win the war," he told a newsreel interviewer at High Wycombe. "My reply to that is that it has never been tried yet. We shall see."[16]

Harris knew that one couldn't fight a war with kid gloves on. Contemptuous of the other two services (he had once snorted that the Army would never realize the value of the tank until it was modified "to eat hay and to shit"), he felt that the average service chiefs were trying to keep this a gentleman's war and that they were far too "pansified" in their attitude to the Boche. After his experiences in Palestine in 1938, when the British Mandate troops were fighting both Jew and Arab, Harris had been even more confirmed in his views. "For the British forces there," he wrote derisively, "the rules . . . amounted to this: you must not get rough, no matter how rough the 'enemy' is. . . . If you get rougher and kill a noticeable number of his men, even if only with the aim of saving your own men, it is just too bad for you."[17]

Most of his young bomber crews had never set eyes on Harris, for he never visited operational stations, but they shared his ruthless attitude to the enemy. Although, in later years, many of them came to have doubts about the bombing of enemy civilians and non-military targets, at the time only a handful of them ever spoke out against such objectives. One young rear-gunner who said over the intercom to his skipper that "I feel sorry for those poor sods down there" was told harshly, "*Well, if you do, fucking well jump out and join 'em!*"[18]

As revealed in a report presented to the Air Ministry in that year, which was based on an analysis of aircrew letters opened by the censors,

They [the letters] illustrate the effect of the aircrews' remoteness from their attacks on human beings. Expressions of satisfaction that the Germans are having to undergo the punishment they have hitherto meted out to others are found in almost all letters, but there is an absence of vindictiveness or fanaticism in the phrases used.[19]

Now "the Chief Bomber", as his new friend Winston Churchill called him, started to ponder what he might do after Lübeck and Rostock. Tucked away in his High Wycombe headquarters, which his chaplain, the Reverend (later Canon) John Collins, considered "perhaps the most soul-destroying, the most depressing of the places in which I had to serve", [20] Harris realized he had to escalate his bombing attacks. No matter what the Luftwaffe had done to Exeter and Bath and what it might do to other British cathedral cities, his concern was to demonstrate to friend and foe alike the destructive capability of Bomber Command.

As he later gloated over the destruction of Rostock, "It took four attacks on four successive nights of moon and clear weather to wreck the town, and only twelve aircraft were missing out of a total of 521 sorties."[21] The result had been 70 per cent of the *Aldstadt* destroyed and some 6,000 civilians killed or seriously wounded, the highest German casualty list so far in the three years of war.

There had to be some means of delivering a single crushing blow, a kind of aerial Waterloo which would bring the enemy to his knees, one which would be followed by a succession of similar massed raids that could only end in defeat for Germany. But where could Harris find the aircraft for such a tremendous raid? Up to now neither side, German or British, had been able to launch more than 500 aircraft on a single raid. Apart from the many technical and navigational difficulties of flying such a huge force to an enemy target, there had always been a problem finding enough aircraft for such a knock-out blow. On paper both the Luftwaffe and Bomber Command could boast thousands of bombers. But they were dispersed over many fronts, split up into training commands and hampered by the large number of aircraft which were always being repaired or being tested for airworthiness.

Like Lord Trenchard, the founder of the Royal Air Force, Harris dreamed of knocking the enemy out of the war by demolishing his factories and killing his civilians. But how could he achieve such a dream? That April, even on paper, Bomber Command's total front-line strength was only 350; that was 150 planes fewer than the Germans had launched against London on that dark December day when Harris had sworn revenge.

But, unknown to Harris, his staff officers—who not only feared him but loved him too: "We would have crawled on our hands and knees," one stated later, "from High Wycombe to London had he asked us"[22]—were already beginning to look into that problem: how to field the overwhelming force Harris needed. They had started making discreet enquiries throughout the country, wherever they knew bombers were stationed, not only the front-line units in Yorkshire and East Anglia but also conversion groups and training commands. They even went so far as to approach their detested rival, the Fleet Air Arm. Even Coastal Command, that vital weapon in the life-or-death struggle against the U-boats, was not sacrosanct.

Slowly the rumours began to multiply and spread, for the operation soon to come was perhaps one of the worst-kept secrets of the Second World War. In the pubs frequented by the off-duty aircrew, such as the Bell in Norwich and Betty's Bar in York, where they drank to forget their fears, sang those bawdy songs about "living off the earnings of a high-born lad-ee" and hoped to find some willing female for the night, there was hasty, whispered, excited talk over the pints and the "shorts" of those who were more "flush" than the rest. The brasshats were in a flap. They were pulling in leave men, rookies, awkward squads—anybody who could fly and man a kite. There was a really big op in the offing.

SIX

Mention Norwich and most people instantly think of its beautiful medieval cathedral or of Colman's mustard. So it is today, and so it was in April, 1942. The mustard was still being produced, although ham had long disappeared. Soon Colman's mustard would, too.

Unlike the other cathedral cities attacked in the Baedeker raids, Norwich had already seen its fair share of action. From the summer of 1940 onwards, in spite of the fact that the coast was well protected by Pile's gunners—"Thirty thousand bloody AA guns," as one of them complained afterwards, "and all we ever shot down was some bloody ducks!"[1]—German raiders swept over the flat washes of East Anglia almost daily to attack the city and the surrounding area.

Between July, 1940, and the same month in 1941, Norwich had suffered twenty-seven air raids; 81 citizens had been killed and 300 wounded. As local photographer George Swain later commented: "I remember Londoners staying here who said they were glad to go home for the weekend and get some sleep."[2]

Indeed, because the city itself was completely undefended—there were no military targets here, unless you counted the food factories—the locals who saw Heinkels and Dorniers streaking across the city almost daily, considered an attack on Norwich to be a "milk run" for inexperienced Luftwaffe pilots: a kind of low-key and not very dangerous combat training mission.

One result of this constant attention by the Luftwaffe, however, was that Norwich was better prepared for civil defence than any of the other Baedeker target-cities. There was, for example, an auxiliary support group, covering 15,000 streets, yards and courts, and manned by some 2,000 women volunteers.

65

There was also an extensive fire-watching system, 12,000 men and women having registered for the task, with an additional 2,500 being issued with compulsory fire-watching notices. In the event, only 180 of these notices were returned; but it was only later that the authorities realized there had been something quite significant in this lack of enthusiasm to do one's duty in case of a raid.

Norwich also had a Q-site. "Q" was a deception device, named after the Q-ships that lured German raiders to attack them, and a Q-site was usually built to resemble a harbour installation or dock, being equipped with cranes, oil tanks, gantries etc. When danger from the air was imminent, the officer in charge set light to prepared bonfires and smoke canisters to make it appear to the German bomber crews that this was the target—and that it had already been hit. But the Q-site could cause problems for the local inhabitants as well as enemy aircrews. The one in nearby Ipswich was used only once, during an exercise, when the excessive smoke generated by the fires blanketed the city for a whole day and sent scores of spluttering citizens to hospital.

Norwich was well equipped with shelters. Some of them, such as the Andersons dug in the garden and the indoor Morrisons, did sterling work in what was to come. But the brick-and-concrete shelters constructed in the streets of terraced housing, where there were no gardens in which to build an Anderson, were widely shunned by the population. They were damp and smelly, often used as unofficial public conveniences and were reputed to fall over like a pack of cards when hit by blast.[3] Just how unpopular they were is revealed by the story of the Dutchman Ter Braak, a sorely tried German agent on the run, who committed suicide in a street shelter in Cambridge in November, 1940. His skeleton was not discovered until the *following spring*.

But Norwich hadn't suffered a serious raid since mid-1941, and the city's defence had become lax. Fire-watchers tended with increasing frequency not to turn up for duty. New recruits to civil defence, replacements for those entering the services, refused to attend training sessions during their non-working hours. If they had to be trained it should be done during the day, they insisted, and they had to be paid for the time they sacrificed. This was in sharp contrast to Germany, where since 1939 every household was forced by law to provide one fire-watcher—without pay—and woe betide anyone who failed to appear for his spell of duty.

It is perhaps also significant, in this lull before the storm, that the number of conscientious objectors in Norwich was increasing alarmingly. Although county councillors and even trade union officials demanded that these "conchies" be dismissed from their council jobs, and the trade unionists stated contemptuously that their lads wouldn't work with these "spineless creatures", the figure rose and rose. In the end, Norwich seems to have had the greatest number of "conchies" in the whole of the United Kingdom and for a while the local newspapers carried a great deal of correspondence for and against them. But that was *before* the Baedeker raid. Many would later harden their hearts to those who wouldn't fight. The people of Norwich were about to experience the realities of war.

When the sirens started at eleven o'clock on Monday night, 27 April, 1942, few of Norwich's citizens were particularly alarmed. They had all heard about the Baedeker raids on Exeter and Bath, and outside a bright "bombers' moon" was shining. But the sirens had sounded often enough before, bombs had been dropped and, as far as they knew, they were well protected. Somebody might be unlucky and "buy one" but that would be about all. Norwich would survive, as it had survived the fifty-odd raids which had gone before. It was probably just another German bomber that had strayed off course.

It had been a beautiful spring day, remembers Mrs B. H. Pettit. Her children were already in bed and fast asleep when the sirens started to wail. Her husband flung himself into his Home Guard uniform and was just whispering goodbye to her, careful not to wake the children, when there was a sudden rattle of machine-gun fire.

"What that?" Mrs Pettit asked, suddenly frightened.

Before her husband could reply, there was a "loud long crunch" followed by more machine-gun fire getting closer by the instant.

"Get the children under the table!" her husband shouted.

Hastily they bundled the children, now alarmed and tearful, under the stout oak table and covered them with an eiderdown. And then, as their old cat crept under the table with the children, her husband left for duty. Mrs Pettit had "a sudden and terrible feeling that perhaps none of us would ever see the beauty of the morning."[4]

She would, but many in Norwich would not.

As the first German planes sailed over the city, dropping their Christmas-tree flares, apparently invincible, one frightened woman scuttled for her shelter and found it already occupied. Her little black-and-white dog Scamp crouched there, trembling. As always, reported Mrs Holmes later, "he had known of the raid before me and now he set off howling miserably".[5] Clutching the dog to her, Mrs Holmes sat in the shelter wondering what was to come.

Some went into the coming battle almost joyfully. One young ARP messenger, John Grix—he was only fifteen but had falsified his age to sixteen so that he could join the Civil Defence—swung himself onto his big sit-up-and-beg bicycle, as the roar of approaching engines grew ever louder. "Come on, Dad," he shouted to his father who was in the Home Guard and was hurrying off to duty, *"it's started!"*[6]

By the time young John returned home, forty-eight hours later, he would have survived bomb blast, machine-gunning and splashing with sulphuric acid, and for his remarkable bravery he would later be awarded the British Empire Medal, perhaps the youngest recipient of that honour in the Second World War.

The bombs had already started to fall. Norfolk Hospital was hit. At Colman's Mustard Factory workers on night shift were decimated by flying shrapnel. A party of ATS, just arrived on a new posting, became victims of a direct hit, a mass of flying arms and khaki-clad legs. Never again would they sing *"She'll be wearing khaki bloomers when she comes."*

A young girl, fifteen years old, was walking home with her mother from the Lido dance-hall in Aylsham Road, the moon so bright that they did not need their torches, when she saw two German planes swoop low over Dolphin Bridge. Bombs started to tumble from their bellies.

"Down!" she shrieked to her mother.

Thereafter, with bombs exploding all around them, masonry falling and tall buildings shaking under the impact like stage back-drops, they pelted for the safety of a shelter. It was strangely empty, but the only thing that mattered was that they now had a thick concrete roof over their heads. So they crouched there, hands over ears, trying to blot out the racket, slowly sensing that the place was getting warmer and warmer. The heat was becoming stifling. For an instant they removed their hands from their ears and touched the wall behind them. The walls were burning! Another explosion. Their hands flew back to their ears.

But even so they could not drown out the sound of flames crackling outside. They knew they couldn't stop inside the shelter, and reluctantly ventured out. The whole area was ablaze. A local shoe factory was on fire and burning woodwork was falling all around the shelter. They fled, with the melting tarmac sticking to their heels. Everywhere people were doing the same, jumping over piles of bricks, dodging the timbers crashing down.

Then the girl came across the most terrible sight she saw in the whole war. Out of the choking smoke clattered a terrified horse, eyes glazed with terror, coat covered with a foam of fear, as it bolted by them pursued by those all-consuming flames, disappearing once more into the smoke like some hideous vision from a nightmare.

Photographer George Swain, braving the bombs to get a scoop, was another who encountered the flames that Monday night. As he cycled through the burning streets he saw "smoke and flames rising. Flares were hanging in the sky and red tracer bullets were making spurts and lines of fire everywhere. Bombs were whistling down." One bomb, in fact landed so close that it flung him from his bike. "Something that felt like a sandbag slumped on top of me and said, 'Sorry old man.'"[7]

But nothing could stop the intrepid photographer, who in all his career had never experienced such a dramatic night as this. Winded and not a little scared, he hopped back on his "trusted iron steed" and set off once more for the scene of the action.

Someone else who had to conquer his fear this night was Home Guardsman Mr A. Percy. Recently discharged from the Army, Percy was now the weapons training officer for the local Home Guard. As such he always carried his 1918-vintage rifle with him, on or off duty. Now, as the bombs fell all around the Michelin tyre depot where he worked, he rushed out to spot "a German plane so low that I could see the reargunner". The target was too tempting. He doubled back to his car where he kept his rifle.

As the plane circled slowly, Percy took aim. With practised ease he took first and second pressure. Then he fired. In that very same instant the plane dropped its bombs. The blast wave slapped him across the face like a blow. Automatically he closed his eyes. When he opened them again, the tyre depot had vanished and the area all around him was blazing fiercely. But forty-odd years later, Mr Percy, now in his seventies, still wonders, *Did I hit the devil or didn't I?*"[8]

Young John Grix had already journeyed two miles through the heaviest bombing, being blown off his bicycle repeatedly by the blast, dodging the spluttering white flames of incendiaries lying everywhere in the débris-littered streets. Once, as he raced by a burning building, bent over the handlebars of his bike as if he were in a cycle race, a vat of acid had exploded over him, spraying his hands with the corrosive liquid. But he had not mentioned the injury to his supervisor at the duty centre. Instead he had volunteered immediately to return through the blazing inferno to lead a group of firemen to a fire; drafted in from another area, the firemen needed a guide.

So, time and time again, dodging in and out of shattered, burning streets, trying to ignore the pain to his burnt hands, John Grix led the fire crews to one fire after another, never uttering a word of complaint. There would be time to have his hands attended to when all this was over, he told himself. But the end of the raid was not yet in sight.

With no guns or fighters to stop them, the twenty-five German aircraft which took part in the first Baedeker raid on Norwich had a field day. They bombed relentlessly. The first two waves of ten aircraft each showered an area of small terraced houses with high explosive bombs. Savagely the humble working-class houses were ripped apart. Gas mains exploded. The fiery flames silhouetted the harassed firemen who attempted to fight the blazes on all sides.

Then the railway station became the city's first major casualty. It burst into flames at once, illuminating the city centre perfectly for the attackers. Clark's shoe factory followed, then MacIntosh's Caley chocolate factory. As one aged cynic said at the time, the burning streets provided "the best fireworks display since Queen Victoria's Jubilee".

Now, as an eye-witness described it, "There was the noise, the screams, the falling bombs, the strange rending moans that timber beams make as they tear themselves apart, the cries of frightened children, and the sound of ambulance bells,"[9] as, relentlessly, the German bombers released their loads of doom.

That night three more members of the Civil Defence won the British Empire Medal for bravery in the face of the enemy. One of them was PC Stockdale, who, although he saw his own home destroyed by a bomb and was under "considerable mental strain", as the official commendation put it, still carried on his rescue duties, not knowing whether his wife was dead or not.

It was not just the men who proved their valour that terrible night. Women did too. The nurses of a local hospital, where incendiaries were dropping "by the hundred" and threatening to burn the place down, evacuated their patients to the surrounding gardens. According to the hospital matron, the patients were equally brave: "Many of these patients were acutely ill," she told the local reporter the next day, "but I did not hear as much as a whimper."[10]

A maternity home filled with young mothers and day-old babies received a direct hit, killing a warden. The matron herself had a narrow escape and later told the press, "My tin hat blew off and the house seemed to fall about us." All the same, she too was full of praise for her patients. "They behaved beautifully, but then you are talking about mothers. . . . They have a highly developed sense of protection and are always calmest in emergencies such as these."[11]

A well-known local boys' school, King Edward VI Grammar School, was showered by incendiaries. But the boys rallied to the emergency and their headmaster later praised their courage in the face of fire all around. "They were magnificent," he said. "The whole place seemed to be alight and the boys running out of their dormitories got to work on the fire immediately. After the NFS took over, they helped to fight fires on the roof of a church."[12]

Other were not so valiant, however. As the local historian records: "When [the fires] engulfed them, many fire-watchers took cover and it needed courageous wardens to encourage their less experienced companions to action."[13] One doesn't need much imagination to visualize how they were "encouraged". But the wardens and fire-fighters had more serious problems to face now than their cowardly colleagues. The water supply was beginning to fail.

The city's mains had been struck early on in the attack. There was water enough in Norwich's two rivers, the Wensum and the Yare, but the means of pumping and delivering it were gone. So it was that before Caley's chocolate factory was hit, its fireguards made full use of the available water to douse a fire at an adjacent premises, but when their own plant was hit, there was no water left.

Once again, the local authorities had been too complacent or too parsimonious to ensure that the city had enough static water tanks—reservoirs of water placed at strategic locations for just such an emergency. A further problem faced the desperate firemen; casting around for any possible source of water, they found they could not get into local houses where there might be a supply because the owners had fled, locking their doors behind them and taking the keys with them. In the end there were 179 fires recorded by dawn.

Shortly after midnight, the bombing became so intense that the night supervisor of Norwich's Telephone Exchange, one of the city's key communications sites, ordered the evacuation of the top storey switchboard. Almost simultaneously there was a knock-out hit on the Eastern Exchange with its trunk lines to Cambridge, site of the Regional Civil Defence headquarters which directed the area's defence. For nearly twenty hours the city would be virtually cut off.

*

Inspector Gerald Sambrooke-Sturgess of the Norwich Special Constabulary had just survived being carried bodily into the air and flung against a wall by the blast of four bombs exploding a hundred yards away when he was told to investigate a report that some people living in a caravan behind the Hippodrome Theatre were trapped there. When he reached the scene he found the theatre itself had been hit. Groping his way through the smoke, he found himself on the stage. Then the part-time policeman had the strangest experience of his whole career in the force. "As I was looking round there was a terrifying noise almost in my ear and my tin hat rose at least an inch off my head! I thought that it must have come from one of the trapped people."[14]

But that wasn't the case. The strange sound had come from a performing sea lion trapped in its cage! With the bombs still dropping all around him, the Inspector went to look for the animal's owner. With no success. In the meantime, however, he did find his way out to the theatre's backyard and discovered "four people in an Anderson Shelter, very dead, jammed together like sardines and covered with dust and rubble".[15] As he could not do anything for the dead—one of whom was presumably the owner of the sea-lion—the Inspector left them there, not knowing he was also leaving behind a fortune for any would-be looter. For he had other problems on his mind; what was he going to do with the sea-lion?

Soon after the Inspector's departure, the shattered Hippodrome had another visitor: the intrepid photographer George Swain. He later recorded the scene of destruction, concluding with this pathetic story:

> From inside the theatre came a terrible sound—wailing, worse than the whistle of a bomb. It was one of the sea-lions which the bomb had released. I shall never forget the noise it made, flapping its ungainly way through the empty theatre crying for its master.[16]

Ten minutes later the first Baedeker raid on Norwich was over. It had lasted exactly ninety minutes and had killed 162 people and injured another 600, with 84 men and women still trapped underneath the smoking rubble. Of the city's 37,000 houses 1,487 were destroyed and 19,600 were damaged in one way or another. But the authorities had learned the lesson of Bath. As soon as dawn broke over the stricken city, they sent loud-speaker vans to tour Norwich. Slowly the vans nosed their way through the pitiful columns of civilians leaving the city down Ipswich Road, pushing their possessions in barrows, handcarts and prams, while the loud-speakers appealed to any fire-watchers and civil defence workers who were going with the refugees to stick to their posts. For the raiders might well return that night.

General Pile reacted swiftly too. Even as the vans were making their appeal and several thousand civilians made homeless by the night's raid began to queue up for new ration cards to replace the ones they had lost, Pile's anti-aircraft guns and balloon barrage team were already on the way to the defence of Norwich. And this time Pile had guessed right.

Two Junkers 88s began to reconnoitre the city from a height of 22,000 feet. For those in the know, their presence meant only one thing: the Germans would come again!

But for the great majority of the city's population, this grey Tuesday morning meant attempting to restore some degree of normality to their lives. At the Norvic Dairy on Dereham Road, the only shop to survive for many streets around, the owner and his wife came out of their shelter to find a small queue of people already forming. They wanted to buy their rations for breakfast. The couple swept away the broken glass from their shattered shop window and started serving through an open window frame.

They would serve thus for hours, until an errand boy struggled by with the basket on his bicycle filled with daffodils which he hoped to sell to a florist in the city. But the way ahead was impassable, so he sold them to the Dairy instead. And, remarkably, there was a rush to buy those daffodils, as if they were a symbol of hope and colour in this time of despair.

But there was nothing beautiful about the task facing Inspector Sambrooke-Sturgess this dawn. He had been told by the regular station sergeant that relatives of the dead sea-lion tamer had mentioned that he and his wife probably had valuables about them. The Inspector thus took upon himself the grisly task of searching the bodies, now reposing in coffins in a nearby cellar.

The information had been correct. The Inspector opened the coffin and discovered that the tamer's wife had a large solitaire diamond ring on her finger—and £600 in bearer bonds stitched into her corsets! But that was not all. Round the tamer's stomach the Inspector found a body belt. He opened it and started to count the large white £5 notes it contained. They totalled exactly £11,000!

Having dealt with the tamer, the Inspector had one more problem to solve. As he later commented, "Coping with that large excited sea-lion in an air raid was not an everyday event. Since its owners were dead a new home was needed—other than the river!"[17] And in due course the animal was sent to a zoo in Scarborough. It seemed well enough, but like many humans it had apparently never forgotten the horror of that Baedeker raid on Norwich; it later died of heart failure during a thunderstorm.

That grim Tuesday saw the start of the gruesome business of identifying the dead at the local undertakers. The corpses had been brought in during the raid, often mangled and caked in blood, and dumped unceremoniously on the floors. Now sobbing relatives filed by, trying to ignore the smell, and attempted to recognize them.

But some were merely gory bits and pieces, incomplete torsos that defied identification. In the end it was ten days before all were satisfactorily named and buried in the mass grave at Earlham Road Cemetery. By then the 162 dead of the first raid had been joined by a further 68 men, women and children.

Another problem requiring urgent attention that morning was the unexploded bombs. Near the Cathedral, built in the Middle Ages at the instigation of Bishop de Losinga, over 500 incendiaries had fallen in two closed containers. The hard-pressed Cathedral fire-watchers had successfully dealt with eight fires that had been set alight on the Cathedral roof and Triforium; now they found themselves confronted with a new menace.

But, in spite of the problems, the city carried on. At the long-established family drapery shop of R. H. Bond & Son at All Saints' Green, an ever hopeful housewife surveyed the ruins of the shop and then asked the manager whether there would be a salvage sale. The manager shook his head sadly and answered, "Madam, there is not enough left to have a sale with!"[18]

Mrs B. H. Pettit, who, despite her premonition, had survived, found Norwich a very different place after the raid. For one thing, there was no electricity or gas and she had to join a queue outside the Co-op to collect water in a pail. On her return home she was met by her mother, who'd just had an eye operation the day before; she'd been brought home from hospital in the car of the very surgeon who had operated on her. "The hospital was hit badly last night and I thought she'd be better off with you," the surgeon explained to Mrs Pettit.[19]

Later Mrs Pettit would reflect: "How grateful we were and how glad to be united after what had only been a few hours but seemed an eternity. Never again shall I judge time by the clock, but by its quality and its contents."[20]

Others had no time for reflection. Their concerns were more

mundane. Although the premises of the Norwich Union Insurance company had been badly hit, the clerks there were inundated with enquiries and claims.

Many people decided to leave the city. It was always the same after a big raid. Mrs Holmes and her little dog Scamp were among them. She had lost her house, so she joined the trekkers, most of them women, who spent the next night on a nearby golf course; they thought it would be safe there if the Jerries returned. One of Mrs Holmes's companions was a pregnant girl, who was making heavy going of the trek. Eventually she could walk no further, and the women tried to flag down an army lorry driver to take the girl to the nearest village. He refused to stop, however, and drove past with the women booing and waving their fists at him in rage.

Suddenly he changed his mind—he must have seen their angry reaction in his rear-view mirror. He hit his brakes. The women raced to catch up with him and pulled back the tarpaulin that covered the back of the lorry, only to gasp with shock. Now they understood his reluctance to take passengers. For there in the back lay "a huge live bomb which the driver had been ordered to take into the country for exploding—at double-quick time!"[21]

Not all fled, of course. People like nineteen-year-old office worker Barbara Dowdesdale were determined to get to work, come what may. So Barbara boarded her usual number 89 bus for the journey into Norwich city centre where she worked. The bus was diverted so many times by signs stating "Road Up" and "Unexploded Bomb" that she began to think "it was all like a board-game of go back and start again". But in the end she reached her office, as did most of her colleagues, "some dirty and all heavy-eyed, but all glad to see each other alive again".[22]

Such citizens, determined to carry on despite all the alarming rumours—"I hear Woolworths has gone for a burton. . . . St Benedict's has had it bad. . . . There's been a lot of people killed in the shelter in Chapel Field Gardens"—were perhaps in a minority that morning. But they were the ones who kept Norwich functioning and cheerful. One story, widely reported at the time, told of two window-cleaners surveying the shattered glassless windows in the city centre that morning. "Cor," remarked one, "we'll probably have to go and sign on at the dole tomorrow!" This wry attitude seemed to exemplify Norwich's determination to battle on, whatever the cost. But there was one rumour that nobody could ignore: *"They'll be coming back tonight."* And everybody in Norwich knew who "they" were.

SEVEN

In fact, the Germans did not return to Norwich that Tuesday night. If they had, they'd have found that things had been moving very fast that day. First General Pile had rushed a mobile battery of eight 3.7 inch guns to Norwich, then a Z-rocket battery—one of "Pile's mattresses", as they were called—and the rocket-firing projectiles were hastily distributed about the city. They might not be very effective at shooting down German aircraft, but impressive they were. Soon even the most timid citizen would venture out during a raid to see the fiery rockets hurtle into the night sky.

The arrival of the guns did wonders for the shaky morale of the townspeople, aided by the fact that Tuesday night passed without incident. But on Wednesday, when unextinguished fires were still smouldering at places like Boots, Woolworths and Caley's, some began to feel anxious again. After nightfall, the glow from those fires would attract enemy bombers like wasps to a honeypot. So, as evening came, thousands of the faint-hearted again began to leave the city. Those who stayed behind must have regretted their decision when, at exactly ten minutes after eleven that night, the sirens started.

They packed the bits and pieces they needed for the shelter, grabbed their gas masks and perhaps a large saucepan to cover their heads against shrapnel, and bolted outside. The moon shone in a cloudless sky. Worse, there was a fresh breeze rising—just what the German fire-raisers needed for their incendiaries. The 20mph wind would be ideal for spreading the conflagration.

This time the leading Heinkels of the famed KG 100, stationed at Chartres, came in from the north-east to avoid the anti-aircraft guns at Yarmouth. Dropping their flares over the still smouldering city,

76

they were soon followed by the main force, from Chievres in France and Soesterberg and Schiphol in Holland. At precisely twenty-five minutes after eleven they started bombing.

Photographer George Swain, out as usual in the middle of the action, thought this raid even more spectacular than the Monday night one:

> There seemed to be fewer high explosive bombs but a far greater number of incendiaries. They dropped in their thousands. Some went through the roofs of houses to start fires inside. Others glanced off the roof to burn themselves out in streets and gardens, or rolled down the tiles and burned in the troughs until the troughs melted. In some districts, mostly containing the homes of working people, there was hardly a street without one fire or more. . . . There was no doubt that the Germans had set out that night to destroy the city, and it looked as if they were succeeding.[1]

Swain was not far wrong. A great blaze had engulfed the whole of the city centre. From Orford Place to Rampanthall Street the fires rose higher and higher. The water mains burst. The firemen were unable to stop the flames reaching St Stephen's Church. Another tremendous blaze engulfed Cuthbert's Printing Works, and there was no water left to put it out. Caley's burned once again and the huge stocks of chocolate resting in the factory melted and started to stream like a great flood of lava into the street outside. Everywhere there was nothing but fire.

Later the authorities reported that there were "very few people in Norwich streets, but the stout hearts who were did excellent work".[2] The reason for the lack of fire-fighters was plain. Most had lost their nerve. They had fled for the cover of the shelters, which themselves quivered and trembled like live things under the impact of the high explosive bombs.

This time the shelters were packed. It was recorded that the Anderson shelters—two slats of curved corrugated steel, joined at the top and covered with earth—survived many close calls that night, with high explosive bombs exploding only yards away but leaving the occupants unharmed. According to one report, however, an elderly woman died of shock, and "several hundred pounds' worth of prize pigeons, which were some of the finest in the country"[3] were destroyed outright.

It wasn't only pigeons that were killed that Wednesday night. Again the casualties were mounting rapidly. In one case, the people sheltering in a Morrison (named after the then Home Secretary, it consisted of a tough metal cage erected inside the house) were trapped beneath tons of rubble and were slowly *grilled* to death by the tremendous heat. In another case, the complete Morrison, together with it occupants, was hurled out of a house by the force of an explosion; it was smashed against the wall of another house, as if by the hand of a petulant giant, then burst open to reveal that everyone inside was dead. By the end of the night the casualties had risen to 68 dead, 86 seriously injured and a further 112 less seriously wounded. Together with the casualties from the previous Baedeker raid, this meant that Norwich had suffered 847 casualties in only forty-eight hours.

The high wind which had been rising all the time swept the flames down the streets like a blowtorch. One cynical observer, noting that hundreds of houses had been razed to the ground, thought that it was "a slum clearance in advance", but wondered at the same time: "Would it pay to say to Hitler that if another bomb fell on a 'Baedeker town', we should begin to bomb their Baedeker towns such as Worms, Heidelberg, Heilbron, Bonn, Ulm and Rotenburg?"[4]

Little did that commentator know that before the Second World War was over, all those towns, with the exception of Rotenburg, would suffer a far worse fate than Norwich.[5]

At last the German bombers had gone. They had dropped shoals of incendiaries and a recorded thirty-nine tons of high explosive bombs in just twenty-five minutes without apparently losing a single plane, although some of them came down to a few hundred feet in order to spray the streets with machine-gun fire.

Timidly, the first civilians began to venture from the shelters to view this new Norwich, a wasteland of smoking rubble, flecked here and there by the orange-red of blazing fires, the streets littered with debris and burnt-out cars, snarls of hosepipes everywhere as the firemen tackled yet another blaze; and all the while the insistent jingling of ambulance bells, carrying the wounded and dying to the hospitals.

Mrs Pettit was one of the first out. She wanted to know if her mother's house had survived the bombing. Now, as the dawn started to flush the sky, she saw it hadn't. Many years later she put down her memories of that moment.

> Strangely enough I can still remember quite clearly a branch of jasmine, white-starred and sweet-smelling, clinging to the

remnants of a demolished shed, and seeing those pathetic half-filled milk bottles in blitzed pantries exposed to the street, whose owners would never need them again.

And a child's shoe, I remember, lying on the path and a ripped-off front door sprawling across the road. All the tiles on the roofs were standing up as if in hideous surprise.

Trees and palings were flung about and the shattered, cracked buildings had crazily tilted chimneys. It was as though a madman had swept by and the crazed eyes of those poor cats and dogs proved it as they wandered about lost and homeless.[6]

Another civilian wandering among the ruins was the indomitable George Swain:

I remember what a lovely dawn it was, calm and mild with the sun shining pink through the smoke and people with smoke-stained faces walking through ruined streets, glad to be alive but saddened by the destruction of houses and shops that had been familiar from childhood. How still the air seemed![7]

A little later Swain was walking down Dereham Road when he passed a primary school: "There were holes in the roof and all the windows were out, but the children were singing." The ruins and the singing children would remain in his memory to the day he died, "as vivid as any of the pictures I took that Wednesday night".[8] It seemed to symbolize for him the spirit of Norwich fighting against adversity, the innocence of childhood overcoming the inhumanity of man.

Trying to analyse her feelings about those two nights when nearly a thousand of her fellow citizens were killed or injured, Mrs Pettit asked herself what came out of the blitz. Sorrow and grief, of course, but something positive as well:

Friendliness and warm human kindness, such as few of us had known before, burst into wondrous blossoms. . . . Looking back and in spite of everything, the food shortage, the sleep shortage, the continual fear for our loved ones always lurking in our hearts, yet those days bred courage, sharpened our awareness of the joys of living, everything was heightened, and it was indeed a time of greatness.[9]

Thus ended the first week of the three-star blitz. In every case the defenders had been caught off guard. Their various technical devices had been found to be unreliable and no match for the machinations of the German boffins. The authorities at all levels

79

from national to regional had failed to defend their citizens adequately. While Germany already had 40,000 men and women in its *Flakdivisionen*, with a great belt of anti-aircraft guns stretching right across the Reich, General Pile was still having to plead for weapons to defend Britain's endangered cities.

Admittedly Britain was winning the propaganda war. Whereas only a few people in the Allied camp realized that Harris's men were bombing non-military targets such as Lübeck and Rostock, the whole of the West knew that the Germans were bombing cultural targets in Britain with the deliberate intention of killing civilians and destroying architectural treasures. After all, they had admitted it openly themselves! In due course, everyone from the Duke of Kent to Eleanor Roosevelt, the American President's wife, was to visit the bombed Baedeker cities and make the appropriate noises. The bombing of Exeter, Bath, Norwich and the other cities to come would make excellent propaganda for Britain's cause in America and the neutral countries.

But what did propaganda matter to the ordinary men and women of the cities attacked? For the price of a dozen aircraft, the Germans had flown a thousand sorties and destroyed the historic centres of three British cities, killing and wounding several thousand people in the process.

The raids, too, had made a mockery of British local independence and civic self-sufficiency, however much propaganda was pumped out centrally in London about the average citizen's ability to "carry on" and "keep on smiling". Thousands were still wandering the country aimlessly and in Norwich, for example, for the first time the authorities were forced to conscript building labour in order to get repairs to housing done.

As the Ministry of Information's secret reports noted at the time, local authorities were "too easily satisfied with the provisions made and are inclined to ignore public opinion . . . [and] to be on the defensive and unwilling to discuss difficulties".[10] Although the civic authorities had supposedly been prepared since 1939, they still seemed incapable of dealing with the emergencies that inevitably followed a raid. In Norwich, for example, one eighty-year-old woman, homeless, penniless and with only the clothes she stood up in, was forced to beg for pennies to buy a cup of tea; it was nearly a week before the local council could offer her any financial help, and that turned out to be the grand sum of £8.

Yet, on the whole, in spite of the failings and deficiencies of the national and regional authorities, morale was judged to be favourable. One way of assessing morale was by counting the numbers of days lost after a raid by the average worker. In the case of Exeter, Bath and Norwich this loss was reckoned to be two to three days. London thereupon expressed the opinion that morale in the Baedeker cities was "excellent".

Unlike the wholesale breakdown of morale reported from Portsmouth the previous year, where there had been mass absentee-ism, with looting and vandalism reaching "alarming proportions" and the police "unable to exercise control," the citizens of Exeter, Bath and Norwich had accepted their fate apparently meekly, allowing themselves to be slaughtered like tame sheep. Of course, as we have seen, there had been some looting. There had been some hysteria, too, and not just among women and children. In Norwich it was observed that some men among the trekkers leaving the city after the first night had "broken down and cried" when ordered to leave the column and return to their fire-watching duties inside the stricken city.

Back in October, 1941, one of the Ministry of Information's researchers, Stephen Taylor, had concluded, after studying the effects of bombing on morale in the hard-pressed Merseyside area: "There is, at present, no evidence to suggest that it is possible to defeat the people of Britain by any means other than extermina-tion."[11] Six months later another report on morale in Hull and Birmingham, prepared for the Air Ministry by a Dr Stradling, suggested the same. The Air Ministry had wanted Stradling to form an opinion "as to the possibility of bringing about a decisive breakdown in morale in urban districts" by bombing.[12] Stradling discovered that production in both cities had fallen only five percent as a result of the raids. Now the most recent attacks on the Baedeker cities had produced similar results.

The question which ought to have been asked—in view of the high morale still existing in the bombed Baedeker cities—was why bomb German cities on the same basis, if the effect on civilian morale was negligible? Were the Germans more chicken-livered than the English? If they weren't, why should their morale break under the bombing?

But such considerations apparently did not enter the minds of the RAF's top brass. "By the end of April, 1942," the official historian wrote triumphantly, "Bomber Command under the vigorous leadership of Air Marshal Harris had shown not only Britain's Allies, but also her enemies, the tremendous power of the long-range heavy bomber force."[13] As for Harris himself, he wrote afterwards with grim satisfaction: "It took four attacks on four consecutive nights of moon and clear weather to wreck the town [Rostock] and only twelve aircraft were missing out of a total of 521 sorties."[14]

It mattered nothing that the effect of the raids on Rostock and Lübeck was over-estimated. Both cities were in full production shortly after the devastating attacks and morale remained high. Far from losing six to seven weeks of industrial output as the Ministry of Economic Warfare had predicted, the two places were operating at between 80 and 90 per cent of normal within a few days. Even the badly damaged Heinkel factory in Rostock was back in production within weeks. Admittedly the medieval houses of both cities had been gutted, but someone in the planning section at the High Wycombe HQ of Bomber Command had seemingly overlooked the well-known fact that industrial plant was extraordinarily resistant to bombing. It would remain thus almost to the very end of the war; indeed German industry in September, 1944, after years of intensive bombing, was producing far more than in 1940.

Nor was it any use that newspapers such as the liberal *Manchester Guardian* wrote that April, "Sentiment and passion are the poorest military advisers," or that the *Norwich Mercury* could proclaim in a strangely prophetic statement: "If Norwich Cathedral were destroyed, it would be no answer to bomb Cologne Cathedral."[15]. The die had been cast. The war of terror in the air was about to escalate even further. Now at last, as Harris had sworn back on that December dawn, the Germans were going to "reap the whirlwind".

PART II

REAPING THE WHIRLWIND

"I do not see why we should always have all the disadvantages of being the gentlemen while they have all the advantages of being the cad."

Winston Churchill, 1944

ONE

It was a typical Tuesday in the middle of the Second World War. A grey day in a grey time. York, which had last been under attack back in 1644 during its great siege, had seen nearly a thousand such grey days. To its shabby, hard-worked, undernourished citizens it was just a day like so many others which had gone before it. There was always a threat of action, even danger in the air, but in the end nothing happened and they would go to their beds and sleep as soundly as they had done every other night since war had begun.

By now the citizens of York had come to regard the hardships and privations of the war as a necessary feature of their lives. Rumour had it there was a thriving black market, but for most of its law-abiding citizens the black market consisted in swapping a quarter pound of sugar, wrapped up in a thick blue bag from the grocer's, with a neighbour over the garden wall for the same amount of tea.

There were plenty of uniforms on the streets, of course—British, Canadian, Polish, even French—and dozens of "good-time girls" hanging around Betty's Bar or parading up and down Coney Street on the look-out for aircrew from Linton, Tockwith, Pocklington and other local airfields. Most of them would not survive their allotted thirty missions and knew it. They were out for fun and the girls were out to give it to them—for a price. There was even talk about "knocking shops" for the Canadians, whose ordinary aircraftmen earned more money than a British officer. At nearby Elvington, soon to be taken over by the Free French, the young Irish MO would lecture new aircrew about the perils of venereal disease, with particular reference to the young ladies they might meet in

York, ending his homily thus: "Now don't forget, chaps, one goirl's as loikely to have 'ut as the next one—if not more so!"[1]

The RAF authorities had tried to put the main rendezvous and trysting place, Betty's Bar, out of bounds for "other ranks". But that didn't stop dashing young pilots taking their NCO crew members and mechanics into the place. The future VC winner, Leonard Cheshire, was one who knew no ranks. "Up guards and at 'em!" he chortled when told Betty's was out of bounds for his men. "We'll sort out any who protest!" Which he did, telling a red-tabbed Army officer who protested: "These men with me have as much right in this place as any of you so-called gentlemen. We work together. We depend upon them. Our lives lie in their hands every other night. . . . I would strongly advise you to go away!"[2] The officer did, and the aircrew celebrated to closing time in a Betty's Bar full of fuming braid and red-tabs.

But for most of York's humble citizens life was simply very humdrum. All they could look forward to was a pint of weak wartime beer in one of the city's many pubs and perhaps a Saturday evening out (after long queuing) at the Regal or the Odeon.

Yet on this particular Tuesday, 28 April, 1942, the drab routine of nearly three years of war was going to be broken at last. Three centuries after Fairfax had trotted triumphantly up to the Minster at the head of his Roundheads and the city had surrendered to the Parliamentary forces, violent action was returning to York. And, had they but heeded it, the city's inhabitants did have advance warning.

At first glance the local newspaper, the *Yorkshire Evening Press*, seemed no different from any other night. Its front page related the usual grim news from Russia and the Western Desert. The American Red Cross, it announced, was going to send "huge cases of new and secondhand clothing" for the city's needy. Nothing at all unusual. Only the leader column on the centre page struck a note of warning. Under the significant headline "*Reprisals*", the un-named journalist wrote:

> The air raids on Bath, followed by the raid on Norwich, remind us of the need to "keep our powder dry" on the ARP "Front". Any night, any place may expect to face a strenuous test of its preparedness and the stamina of its citizens, who, if they are wise, will not lay too much stress on their hitherto surprisingly consistent "run of luck".[3]

The leader writer's advice was aimed quite clearly at York itself, which had suffered 700-odd alarms so far, but only a few bombs, though, nightly, to the east its citizens could see the glow of the fires burning over the hard-pressed city of Hull. Had that unknown journalist, penning his leader in the *Press*'s old-fashioned offices next to the city's ancient Guildhall, known something? Was he aware that General Pile's mobile gun column was already racing towards York? We will never know, for he is long dead. But one thing is certain. York's run of luck had ended.

Now it was nearly midnight. The old city was virtually deserted. Like the several score of other "enemy aliens" in York—German, Austrian, Italian—Elisabeth X had long since dashed home to beat the police curfew. The pubs and cinemas were closed. Soldiers and airmen from the surrounding camps were on their way back, trying to reach the guardroom before the magic hour of 2300 hours. If they didn't, they'd be on a "fizzer" the following morning.

Here and there a few people were awake. At his post to the east of the city, insurance agent and ARP man Jack Popplewell told his mates, "Lads, I have a funny feeling we're gonna cop it tonight."[4] His colleagues agreed with him. They all went to bed in their bunks, fully dressed save for their boots. It was well they did so. This night they would really "cop it".

On the other side of the River Ouse, which meandered through the sleeping city, three middle-aged citizens walked down the moonlit street of Bootham, flanked on both sides by elegant Georgian houses. They had spent an enjoyable evening finishing off a whole bottle of precious whisky between them. For one of them, the city's coroner, Colonel Innes Ware, it was a little like the old days in the Great War. As a young officer in the trenches he had easily downed half a bottle of scotch. Now he was happily tired, ready for bed.

One of his companions, however, the headmaster of the nearby public school, St Peter's—which had educated that most notorious fire-raiser of all, Guy Fawkes—was a little apprehensive. He looked at the full moon and commented: "It would be a lovely night for a reprisal raid, Innes, wouldn't it?"

Colonel Ware, who was also head warden for the Bootham area, groaned, "*Please!* I'd like to get a good night's sleep tonight."[5]

With that they parted to go their separate ways. When they met again, they would have suffered the full horrors of total war. Loyal comrades would have been killed before their horrified eyes, and the headmaster would suffer the heartbreak of seeing his school set alight by some latterday Guy Fawkes from the air.

It was midnight. The city was silent. The stage was set and the drama could begin.

Oberfeldwebel Hans "Sepp" Fruehauf, a giant of a man, had sneaked away from his home on the Moselle back in the '30s to join the newly emergent Luftwaffe as a regular. In those days Germany west of the Rhine had been unoccupied since the Allied occupation armies had left in 1930, and young men were not called up for the *Reichswehr*. But as an eighteen-year-old Hans had never fancied the humdrum life of a provincial Moselle township, where everything depended on the annual wine harvest; he had always wanted to be a soldier.

After 1939 he had adventures enough. He had flown as a radio-operator-cum-observer over Warsaw. Twice he had been over London back in 1940. Then had come the campaign in the Balkans, which had been followed by Russia, from whence he had recently escaped with "the Frozen Flesh Order, Second Class" as cynics called the medal given to those who had suffered frostbite. Now he was back in the West, an "old hare" trying to put some backbone into the "greenbeaks" currently training in Holland and France for the great bloodletting of the Russian front. Thus it was that on this Tuesday night he found himself flying over the North Sea, heading for an English city he had only heard of a few hours before—York.

The twenty-odd aircraft zooming in over Flamborough Head were immediately picked up by the underground radar station at Patrington, near the Humber. Warnings were flashed to all local Royal Observer Corps posts to follow the progress of the raiders, for, even as the night-fighters were being scrambled, it was still not known what the Germans' target was.

Now the German bombers raced across the broad acres of Yorkshire, over Driffield Air Field, the first to be bombed in Yorkshire in both wars, with, to their right, the dull glow of a still-burning Hull. For the port had again been raided the previous day: and Fruehauf knew the importance of Hull, through which the supplies to Russia flowed, heading for the port of Murmansk.

There it was, the silver snake of the River Ouse, just as the briefing officer had described it. The attackers came lower. Not a flak gun or fighter anywhere. So much for the vaunted Royal Air Force, Fruehauf told himself. His first raid over England since 1940 was going to be just like a raid in Russia, where the Luftwaffe did virtually what it liked, the Ivan fighter-pilots were so lousy.

1. Lübeck Cathedral is hit.

2. A spire collapses.

3. Victims of the raid on Lübeck.

4. St Martin's Church, Coney Street, York, on the morning of 26 May, 1942.

5. The Guildhall, York, after the raid.

6. Five nuns died when this convent in York was hit on 28 April, 1942.

7. Canterbury Cathedral looking across from St George's Street after the ruined buildings had been levelled and fences put up along the roads.

8. Rescue workers in the wreckage of one of the buildings in the St George's area of Canterbury, 1 June, 1942.

9. St George's Church, Canterbury, wrecked by bombs in the early hours of 1 June, 1942.

10. St George's Street, Canterbury, showing the clocktower of the church, the only part remaining today.

11. The Wincarnis Works, Westwick Street, Norwich, on fire, April, 1942.

12. St Benedict's Gate, Norwich, April, 1942.

13. Exeter Cathedral, seen through an archway after the bombing.

14. Debris blocks Catherine Street, Exeter, behind Colson's store (now Dingles).

15. St Mary's Roman Catholic Church, Julian Road, Bath.

16. Upper Bristol Road, Bath.

17. Cologne; a view of the wrecked bridge from the cathedral.

18. American troops enter Cologne, 6 March, 1945.

19. Bomb damage in Hamburg.

20. Where they flew from. Airfields from which 58,000 young men flew to their deaths disappearing into the undergrowth.

Top: Tockwith

Middle: Long Marston

Bottom: Pocklington

Suddenly Fruehauf craned forward. Towering up ahead, standing out from the plain, was the great silver mass of a huge church. "It was beautiful standing above the city bathed in the moonlight," he recalled many years later. "So close I felt I could almost lean out and touch it."[6]

But as the first flares floated down to illuminate the still sleeping city, Fruehauf forgot the beauty of the place they had come to bomb. There was work to be done.

Museum assistant Violet Rodgers was awakened by an "unpleasant thud" somewhere nearby in the district of Clifton. In that same instant the sirens started to shrill. She sprang out of bed, telling herself it had happened at last. She must hurry to her duty station.

With her friend Dr Alice Lewis, both in helmets now, she rushed outside to find it was "as bright as day". Incendiaries were already burning in the garden and were whistling down all the time. They started to run down virtually deserted streets, which were "lit up by the strange unnatural glare of magnesium from the incendiaries burning on the roofs everywhere".[7]

They reached their duty station safely to find all their comrades in the First Aid Post already lying on the floor "like sardines" and the calm Scottish voice of their chief Dr Moss saying soothingly, over and over again, "Lie down, lassies, while you have the chance. Lie down."[8]

It was a portent of what was to come.

Young Peter Lawson, in the nearby Groves district, also chanced going outside as the bombing started. He had a duty to perform too. It was his task during an air raid to go and pull the string attached to the big toe of "Deaf Mary", a stone-deaf neighbour. Every night she would attach the string and dangle it through her bedroom window so that she could be wakened and taken to the shelter in the event of an air raid. But now as the incendiaries were followed by high explosive bombs, Peter thought better of his self-imposed task. He fled to the safety of his parents' shelter, leaving Deaf Mary to her fate. She survived, sleeping through the whole raid, but on the morrow she would castigate the youngster for not having woken her "in time".[9]

On the other side of town future actress Judi Dench, then an eight-year-old schoolgirl, was wide-awake and trembling, for her parents had still not returned home from a theatrical performance. She and her teenage nurse clutched at each other on the stairs of the cellar as the old house rocked and trembled under the impact of the bombs.

Colonel Innes Ware, rudely awakened from his sleep, left his wife to the task of shepherding their children into the shelter—plus their black labrador Bruce and their three billetees, including one highly nervous Signals officer—and grabbed his bike. He had heard the bombs too and knew how swiftly the fires would spread. Pedalling furiously, he passed his old friend's school, St Peter's, already well ablaze, and raced for his post in Bootham. The incendiaries were dropping all about, but he ignored the danger. His primary concern was to check that his deputy, Mr Colman, was on duty and taking charge of the post.

But Colman was already dead, killed outright by the first stick of bombs which had straddled the nearby railway line. A moment later the middle-aged Colonel, whose eardrums had both been shattered by blast in the First War, nearly suffered the same fate himself as a further stick whistled down. The Colonel flung himself to the ground just in time. The bombing had started in earnest.

Oberfeldwebel Fruehauf recognized the outline of York's elegant LNER railway station, once Europe's biggest, without difficulty. They had been well briefed for this raid. Although the Tommies would later claim the raid on York to be a reprisal one, the Luftwaffe had a definite military objective in mind. If they could knock out the signals system at York, the whole railway network in the north-east would be affected. In particular, the supplies which flowed through Hull to the "Popovs" might be cut off. "Rub out the signalling system," the briefing officer had told them only hours before, "and there won't be much leaving Hull for Murmansk to help the Russians for the next few weeks."[10] And Fruehauf knew that his former comrades on the *Ostfront* needed any help they could get. He concentrated on the curved glass roof of the station, now tinted a dramatic blood-red by the flames, as the pilot took the plane into a shallow dive. They were going in for the attack.

The crowded 10.15 London—Edinburgh train had just steamed into the station as the sirens sounded their warning. But although the assistant station master and the railway police had run up and down the platform, warning the soldiers and civilians in the train to get off and take cover, not many did so. They had fought hard for their places in the train and there was still another 250 miles ahead of them to Edinburgh. So they stuck to their seats or their places in the crowded corridors. There were even soldiers jammed into the toilets and when a child needed to "go", he was passed from hand to hand over the heads of the others until he reached the soldier occupying the seat who did "the necessary".

The first 250lb bomb, striking the far end of the platform, rapidly changed their minds. Everyone dashed for cover as incendiaries began to rain down through the shattered glass roof. The parcels office caught fire, as did the ticket office. Suddenly everything seemed to be burning, including the track and the Edinburgh express.

Women porters, hefty ladies in baggy navy-blue overalls and peaked caps, sprang into action, booting incendiaries from the platform onto the track. Meanwhile the assistant station master and two shunters, aided by some unknown soldiers, fought to divide the train; they eventually managed to back out fourteen coaches, still undamaged, leaving another six blazing inside the station.

But the fires were gaining the upper hand in parts of the station and so, thrifty Yorkshiremen that they were, the booking office staff decided to carry the day's takings to safety. But in what? There was a great heap of silver and coppers. In the end they scooped the contents of the till into an old wellington boot and ran for cover in the nearby Station Hotel. At least the London and North-Eastern Railway wouldn't make a loss on the raid!

While Fruehauf's pilot concentrated on the station itself, other planes swooped low over the railway lines running into and out of it. Some of their bombs inevitably missed the target and struck non-military objectives, though they did come very close to knocking out the signalling system.

One bomb hit the oldest girls' school in the country, the Roman Catholic Bar Convent, just outside one of the bars or gates guarding the city walls, which housed a secret chapel dating back to the days of Catholic persecution. Three nuns were killed outright, including the Mother Superior, and three were trapped in the smoking ruins. Every one of the city's grammar schools, all grouped near the railway, was hit too, as were many of the other schools located in the centre.

One bomb of the stick which struck Nunthorpe Grammar School hit a modest terrace house just behind it. In an instant all was chaos in the crowded house. A major billeted there was flung through the window into the street, and a great chunk of masonry whirled through the roof of the house behind, killing its elderly occupant outright. Then the house collapsed trapping the dead, the dying and the injured.

ARP man Jack Popplewell found himself burrowing deep into the rubble, looking for survivors but with little hope of success; already he had hauled out a dead ATS. Suddenly he heard a moan. Frantically scrabbling away, he found an unconscious woman with a dreadful wound on her forehead. She was still alive, although she would have to spend six months in hospital before she recovered fully. Then Mr Popplewell spotted the child; but —"I knew she was dead straightaway. I called back to my mates at the entrance to the tunnel, don't bother about the nipper. She's snuffed it."[11] Then he continued digging for other survivors.

It was only forty-odd years later that an elderly Mr Popplewell learned that the "nipper" who had "snuffed it" was in fact alive, a healthy woman of forty-three married to an American surgeon with daughters of her own!

Still the Germans pressed home their attack on the railway station. Another wave came in and showered the area of the Carriage Works with high explosive. A roundhouse containing twenty locomotives was hit; every engine was ripped and scarred a bright new silver by the flying shrapnel. The pride of the LNER, named after a former chairman, Sir Ralph Wedgwood, was tossed on its side like a child's toy.

But it wasn't only the railway's "iron horses" that suffered. One bomb landed directly on the stables which housed the LNER's handsome drayhorses (now the site of the National Railway Museum). Stableman Alfred Martin, accompanied by two other men, rushed in. Ignoring the flying hooves of the frightened Clydesdales and Shires, they loosened the halter of each horse and then urged them out of the smoke and flame with a smart slap to their rumps. One by one they were urged out, until Mr Martin, his face blackened with smoke, had freed nineteen of them, and was left to stare ruefully at his "dig-for-victory" garden. It was ruined, his prize cabbages crushed to shreds by the stampeding hooves. At that moment, the sight saddened him more than that of his burning house.

But at last, after an hour in which the city was totally undefended, help was on the way. Leading the night-fighters was a young French pilot, Lieutenant Yves Mahé, who had come a long way for his first battle with the Boche. Back in 1940, when he was only twenty-one, Mahé had stolen a plane just before the Germans had taken his base. Unknown to him, his brother had done the same, and by a long roundabout way the two had finally reached England, where by chance they met on Yves's first day of sightseeing in London.

Now the dark-haired pilot flung his Hurricane straight at an unsuspecting Heinkel III, machine guns blazing. His first burst missed, the tracer alerting the German pilot to his danger. He flung the bomber to the right. Mahé was not to be thrown off. Doggedly he hung on to the German's tail, pumping short sharp bursts into the Heinkel's fuselage. Desperately the German rear-gunner tried to fight him off, but already thick black smoke was pouring from the Heinkel's right engine.

"I gave the Hun a good taste of his own medicine," the triumphant Free Frenchman told reporters the next day. "I fired again and followed the Heinkel as it spiralled down, but near the ground I lost sight of it in the smoke and haze hanging over the city."[12]

Mahé's first "kill" was later confirmed, however, and in due course General de Gaulle awarded him the Croix de Guerre and York's civic leaders welcomed the hero to the Mansion House for tea and cucumber sandwiches.

The dying Heinkel frightened off Fruehauf's pilot just as he was going to drop his last bomb on Rowntree's chocolate factory, which, unknown to him, contained a shell-filling plant that would have caused a tremendous explosion if hit. Instead, he jettisoned the bomb harmlessly near the railway line and fled for the coast. That was the last Hans Fruehauf saw of England until he returned as a tourist on a weekend trip to London thirty years later. The survivors of the Baedeker attacks over Britain found themselves fighting the rest of the war in Russia, Fruehauf among them, as infantry soldiers.

York's city centre was blazing merrily. Roofs were on fire everywhere, including the Guildhall, next to the secret command post from which York's civil defence was directed, and the nearby Theatre Royal, one of England's oldest theatres. At King's Manor, where Henry VII and the ill-fated Charles I had once lived and which was now a school for the blind (today it houses part of York University), the blind children huddled in helpless terror in the ancient cellars. A hundred yards away in blazing Bootham, however, one elderly lady was determined she and her friends were not going to be burned alive. Ignoring the flames, the falling glass, the machine-gunning, old Mrs Martin—she was ninety-one years of age—led a long crocodile of frightened friends from the home in which they lived to the safety of what is now Radio York. And above this scene of death and destruction, in the heart of a city which had been there before the Romans came, the Minster towered, its walls lit up by the flames.

The enemy was leaving now. It was 4.46 am in the secret control post, surrounded by flaming buildings on both sides of the River Ouse, when the exhausted controllers received the code-word *White* meaning "attack over". It had been two hours and ten minutes since the code-word *Purple* had flashed across Yorkshire, meaning "enemy attack imminent". During those two hours of hectic activity the controllers had plotted scores of incidents all over the city, despite coming under direct attack themselves: an incendiary had crashed through the ceiling and the blast of a high-explosive bomb had flung one of the team across the room. At last, as the sirens sounded the All Clear, they could relax with a cup of tea.

The survivors began to emerge from their shelters. The Rev Harry Radcliffe, who had been on duty as a warden with Michael Rennie of the Theatre Royal, the future Hollywood star, wandered into a wrecked Bootham to see if he could help. But the curate didn't get far. Suddenly an irate voice snapped, "Get off my bloody legs!" He flashed his torch downwards and could just make out the figure of a man half-trapped under some rubble. He dug with his bare hands and at last managed to release the man "who didn't have a word of thanks to say to me for my efforts afterwards". Later, when the curate went across to a mobile canteen to buy a cup of tea, he discovered that, even as he'd been struggling to help him, "the old codger . . . had nicked my wallet!"[13] That was not the first or last incidence of theft, looting and petty larceny recorded after the York blitz.

All over the city rescue workers were tunnelling into the smoking rubble to find trapped survivors. Trooper Cooke, on his first leave from the Army, having been called up from his post as head of Civil Defence, now took it upon himself to check if the most sensitive area of the system, which he himself had set up, was functioning. It was the emergency mortuary for the victims, ominously close to the City's slaughterhouse.

Cooke was not an emotional man. All the same, he was stirred by the way that ordinary York men and women stood up to the horrors of the grimly named Bodies Room. Forty years later he remembers that some of the corpses were "pretty ghastly":

> One mother dead with her dead child locked in her arms, the two of them mixed up with brick rubble on a metal stretcher ... In a couple of cases, all that was needed was a bucket to put the bloody remains into.[14]

Trooper Cooke saw more horror this day than he did two years later on active service in Normandy. But now, as he helped with the grisly job of identifying the bodies, he thought "how typically English" everything was, "quiet, subdued and unemotional".[15]

On the other side of the city, Violet Rodgers, the assistant at York's Castle Museum, was appalled at the destruction around her:

> Bootham was a sight to make an historian weep. Glass, glass everywhere, crunching under our feet. Every house had staring empty windows, tiles off the roofs, and the walls all pitted with machine-gun bullets.[16]

Trying to get to work to see if her precious museum had been damaged, she found several streets blocked by fallen masonry from Georgian architectural treasures and by the attendant fire engines and their tangled skeins of hosepipes. It was heart-breaking. Suddenly she stopped. Ahead of her, "gleaming white and undamaged in the sunlight", stood Bootham Bar, one of the four main gates in the medieval town walls. To Violet Rodgers, at that moment, "It was like a symbol of endurance, the continuity between the ancient city's long past and the certainty of the future. *York would endure!*"[17]

TWO

As the weary citizens of York began the long job of picking up the pieces, the Press descended upon them in force. *"The spirit of blitzed York stands very high . . . Nazi fury launched at York . . . Nazi reprisal raid on York . . . Widows gunned in hostel garden"* screamed the headlines that day.[1] Reporters noted "the cheerful faces and the bustle in the streets . . . tradespeople sweeping away glass splinters into neat piles outside their shops".[2] The Lady Mayoress, Mrs Crichton, who had viewed the burning city from the roof of the Mansion House, told one reporter forcefully: "This will *not* win the war for the Germans!"[3] It was all good, patriotic stuff which showed that the citizens of the blitzed city were carrying on bravely, full of Yorkshire grit, typical hard-headed "tykes".

The reality was a little different. Already long queues of people were forming outside the Library to find out the casualties, and outside the Post Office to telegraph news of themselves to loved ones elsewhere. The casualties were high. Some 300 men, women and children within the city's boundaries had been killed or seriously wounded, excluding Army and RAF casualties which were never published, though nearby Clifton Airfield had been hit. Of the prewar total of 28,000 houses, some 9,500 had been destroyed or damaged.

Amazingly, the Minster had not been hit—and this fact was already being broadcast by the BBC, to the horror of some local citizens who thought it might attract the Germans back to finish off the job. As Mrs Crichton said in a wire to Brendan Bracken, the Minister of Information: "The citizens of York are deeply concerned at the reference to the Minster. Request no York building be referred to by name in future communications."[4] Forty years later when the Minster was seriously damaged by fire after a lightning strike, the whole world was shocked. Back in 1942, however, many York people, knowing what a give-away landmark the ancient pile really was, would gladly have seen it blown to smithereens as long as that destruction kept the Jerries away!

It was a day of contrasts. Blood donors rushed to the County Hospital to offer their blood, but were turned away with a severe reprimand from the doctor in charge: "Blood on the shelf is much more valuable to us for keeping up supplies than a deluge of offers after an emergency."[5] Refugees from Hull, meanwhile, were turned back at Beverley by the police, who told them "There is nothing left standing in York".[6] The city itself was flooded with tourists; but they were not there to see the antiquities, they were there to gape at the ruins. In the end the Lady Mayoress had to protest publicly that the victims' suffering was being increased "by the thoughtlessness of some . . . visitors",[7] and the police started posting notices at the entrances to the city, reading, "No sightseers!"

There were contrasting attitudes to the damage too. A spokesman for Guy Fawkes' old school, St Peter's, protested that the school had hardly been hit and that reports suggesting it had been put out of action were wrong, for the school was "in full swing".[8] On the other hand, the Principal of the Blind School at King's Manor protested that "Many people . . . glancing casually at the front of the building have been heard to say, 'Oh, the Blind School has only a few windows broken.' " On the contrary, he maintained: "A beautiful Elizabethan block has been reduced to a mere burned-out shell. And every roof at the back has been terribly damaged by the thousands of stones, large and small, thrown up by the bomb, which burst not far away."[9]

At eleven that morning, in the midst of all the confusion, the delegates of various ministries, the civic authorities and the military filed into the Public Library, past anxious crowds reading casualty lists, and took their places in the meeting room. It was customary procedure all over the country for them to meet after a raid. Their purpose was to discuss what had happened and, if necessary, apportion blame to any department which had failed in its duty. Among the collection of dignitaries, under the chairmanship of the future Lord Harlech, was humble Trooper Cooke in his dusty battledress, devoid of decorations or marks of rank.

But despite his lowly station, Trooper Cooke turned out to be the star of the show, for any question on the conduct and behaviour of Civil Defence would always be referred to him. In the end, an exasperated brigadier from Northern Command was heard to grunt to his neighbour: "Who is that bloody trooper?"[10]

Finally the committee agreed that, with two exceptions (which were never revealed), "It can be said without hesitation that, on the whole, the services and the citizens acquitted themselves well."[11] Undoubtedly the local ARP services and the citizens had done their best—but the Armed Services and the national authorities patently had not. After the other Baedeker raids, as the *Yorkshire Evening Press* leader writer had surmised the previous evening, it had been pretty clear that it would be York's turn soon. Yet when forty enemy bombers had been spotted flying west over Flamborough Head, and as Trooper Cooke put it, "We had no doubt that York was in for it," why were there no RAF fighters waiting for them?

Why had it taken Lieutenant Mahé's lone Hurricane so long to arrive on the scene? Why hadn't General Pile's anti-aircraft guns and barrage balloons come on time? (Ironically, when they did appear, York was never again seriously threatened.) Why was it that, after a week of Baedeker raids, the operators attempting to jam the German signals had still not realized that their sets were defective, so that the Germans came within a hair's breadth of knocking out the vital north-eastern railways signal system? These questions remain unanswered to this day.

But in that spring of 1942, if the average man in the street had his doubts, he kept quiet about them and continued to eke out his existence the best he could. He left the greater issues of the day to his masters.

That morning fiery little Ellen Wilkinson, who had once led a celebrated hunger march from Durham to Whitehall and was now Parliamentary Secretary to Herbert Morrison, the Home Secretary, visited battered Norwich, fighting to recover after its second Baedeker raid. She told the local Press that "the situation was in hand" and that "Norwich people on the streets and in the rest centres are so stoical under their ordeal."[12]

Later she and her boss, who in the First World War had been a conscientious objector, plus Lady Rhondda and the diarist James Lansdale Hodson, discussed the Home Front in general. Severely critical of the War Office, they felt that "the Government should be more decisive about the Britain it wished to build after this war is ended".[13] Miss Wilkinson was also critical of some Army battle-school training methods; one particular school, she said, "fills sacks with blood and squirts mud and blood on men as they thrust their bayonets into the sacks". Morrison agreed that that sort of thing should be kept quiet, but felt that "the authorities believed this training might give the added twenty per cent of fighting spirit that would make all the difference between success and failure".[14]

Lady Rhondda opined that someone—preferably Churchill—ought to tell the people what they were fighting for, adding: "What about convincing people of what will be in store for them *if we lose?*"[15]

But while the socialist planners of 1942 indulged themselves over lunch of smoked salmon and chicken in a private room in the Berkeley Hotel, outside the real shooting war still raged. On every front Britain was still defeated. Secretly, Churchill, the one politician who really understood the issues at stake, ordered that anthrax should be tested for use as a last-ditch weapon on a remote Scottish island. On 10 May he told Germany in a public broadcast on the BBC World Service that he wouldn't hesitate to use gas if Germany employed it first. The Old Man knew perfectly well what would happen if we lost.

As the April of the Baedeker raids gave way to May, the bomber commander Leonard Cheshire found himself put out to pasture. He had been posted to Marston, just outside York, where he commanded a so-called Conversion Unit. "Likely to be at Marston for a long while," he wrote home that May, "turning out Halifax captains by the dozen and at it as hard as ever."[16]

In his spare time Cheshire worked on the proofs of his book *Bomber Pilot*, pondered over a film script and showed off his new American wife to old friends. However, as the then fourteen-year-old painter R. Bell remembers: "He was always on the field, roaring around in his old banger, talking to everybody from the lowest erk right on up. I bet you in those days he put in twenty hours a day—and he never stayed on the ground a moment more than necessary. He was always flying."[17]

All the same, Cheshire was developing a taste for domestic life at his rented home, The Granary, in the village of Linton-on-Wharfe.

> I hope to goodness the war will be over this year. I've given up wanting to go on indefinitely. I'm also scared of a plague of some sort breaking out on the Continent and the thought of Christopher [his brother] locked up there gets on my nerves. Thank God, at least they don't commit atrocities on British prisoners. Reading between the lines I feel the air war will flare up very shortly, but I don't know whether it will lead to greater things.[18]

Cheshire's hope for the war to end in 1942 would not be realized, but his guess that the war in the air would soon flare up and "lead to greater things" was to prove accurate.

It was only a matter of days later that he and his fellow instructors were called to the station commander's office. Here they were told to prepare for a very special operation which would take place during the next full-moon period. The training unit and Conversion Command would provide more than half the aircraft needed. Cheshire, who later founded one of his Cheshire Homes not a dozen miles from where he now prepared for war, went back to his quarters in thoughtful mood. What kind of "op" could this be which needed half-trained rookies to fly it, he wondered. But of one thing he was certain: the next full moon occurred in the last week of May, 1942.

Sunday, 3 May was a fine day in Exeter. The news from the various fronts was desperate; it was defeat after defeat from South-East Asia to North Africa. But the majority of Exeter's citizens were more concerned with home affairs than what was happening on the other side of the world, however awful.

It was now over a week since Exeter had become the first Baedeker target. The locals had grown used to the stark black ruins with their intimate glimpses of disturbed interiors. That morning the last of Exeter's UXBs (unexploded bombs) had been safely removed from its pit in Culverland Road and the inhabitants evacuated from the area could return to discover just how much property they had lost. Even the more fearful citizens, who had taken to sleeping outside the city, were now beginning to drift back to their homes. Now it was generally agreed that the Baedeker bombers had moved north. Exeter had had its share.

Towards evening, a breeze seemed to spring up from nowhere. Those who concerned themselves with such things noted, too, that the evening was exceptionally clear and that the moon was rising. Soon, or so it was said, one could have read a newspaper by the moon's light. But no one worried. The Jerries wouldn't be coming back to Exeter.

They came in over the coast in the early hours of Monday, 4 May, twenty-five to thirty Junkers fighter-bombers. Using the River Exe as their guide, they arrived over their target at exactly one thirty. As Goebbels's spokesman proudly announced a few hours later on Radio Berlin, "We have chosen as targets the most beautiful places in England. . . . Exeter is a jewel!"[19] Now they had come to destroy that jewel.

Wave after wave, the planes swooped over Exeter to drop their bombs. In one of the later planes was *Oberleutnant* Ernst von Kugel, guided to the target by "the bright reflection of fires on the horizon".

> Over the town itself I saw whole streets of houses on fire. Flames burst out of windows and doors, devouring the roofs. People were running everywhere and the firemen were frantically trying to deal with the flames. It was a fantastic, fascinating sight. No one who saw it will forget the greatness of this disaster.[20]

Von Kugel was not exaggerating. The whole city centre—South Street, Fore Street, High Street, Sidwell Street and a dozen others—was ablaze. The fire-watchers and the NFS were swamped. Aid was being rushed to the stricken city from as far afield as Reading. As one helpless fireman gasped, there were "acres of fire".

The City Library, only recently built, disappeared in flame together with a million books. The Cathedral shuddered as one HE bomb struck the roof, destroying three buttresses on the south side, ripping the vaulting off and severely damaging the interior. If another buttress had been destroyed that would have meant the collapse of the whole roof. People later thought it almost symbolic that a huge picture of Christ, fifteen feet by six, had gone untouched. "An angel guided the bomb," they said in awed voices. Even so, damage to the Cathedral was heavy, with lumps of masonry weighing twenty-five tons being flung all over the place. As one man later told the local newspaper, "It will take all of a million pounds to restore the Cathedral, but we shan't see it done in our time—it'll take twenty-five years."[21]

And the human casualties were horrific: 161 killed and nearly 500 injured. But the cold statistics could never convey the true suffering of many Exeter people that terrible night, burnt alive, mutilated by shrapnel, blinded by flying glass, crushed to death by falling debris.

One man, for instance, was admitted to hospital with his overcoat still on. He was conscious but in no apparent pain, though he was suffering from shock and a weak pulse. One hour later he died, still clothed, after a blood transfusion. Finally he was undressed by the hard-pressed young VADs, who reeled back in horror when they now discovered the reason for his strange death—the lower part of his trunk was completely missing.

Such horror, of course, was lost on the German attackers. As von Kugel stated at the time: "We thought of the thousands of men, women and children, the victims of our deadly visit. But we thought of our Führer and the word of command he gave—*revenge*! With cold calculation we carried out our orders."[22]

Another German pilot who later recorded his impressions of the fire raid said: "We were glad when we saw our bombs fall on Exeter, as we were conscious we were fulfilling the Führer's promise to retaliate, blow for blow, for attacks on German towns."[23]

But this time the Germans weren't having it all their own way. That night an unnamed Polish sergeant-pilot scored two kills in quick succession. He was only just airborne when he spotted a Junkers 88, silhouetted against the icy silver of the moon. He didn't hesitate. Just before he overshot the Junkers with his Hurricane, he pressed the firing button. Tracer flew towards the German intruder like a flight of fiery hornets. Pieces of metal were ripped from his fuselage. Almost immediately the Junkers began to spiral ever downwards in its final dive of death, trailing smoke behind it. The Pole, who had come so far to achieve this revenge, watched in fascination. Suddenly there was a burst of flame. Next moment, the bombs and incendiaries which the Junkers had been carrying detonated in one great explosion.

Only minutes later his cannon shells ripped into a second intruder and the young Pole was an instant "ace". He had shot down two German bombers in less than ten minutes!

But still there were others, carrying out their Führer's command, intent upon the ruthless destruction of this "jewel", determined to exact revenge for Lübeck and Rostock. They machine-gunned the General Hospital and set it on fire so that the staff were forced to evacuate the patients, stretchers packed like sardines on the wet grass outside.

The Telegraph Exchange was struck too, and in an instant was a mass of searing flames. The lines went dead, and only then did the telegraphists abandon their posts and scurry for safety. "We tried to get out by way of the emergency stairs," one of them reported excitedly afterwards, "but when we looked out the street was just a sheet of flames. The only other way was up the back stairs. The door leading to them would not open, so we broke it with a hammer, and managed to get out into the side passage and climb over the gates."[24] Some, however, did not escape but died a terrible death as the Telegraph Exchange burned down.

But among the horror there were lighter moments, too. One house received a direct hit and the front wall collapsed to reveal a bed on the first floor, perilously close to a drop of twenty-odd feet—and the bed was still occupied. An ARP warden clambered through the smoking rubble, fearing the worst. But the old man in the bed wasn't dead. He was stone-deaf and fast asleep.

A cyclist was riding through some allotments when he noticed several gruesome patches of red gore on the ground. He shivered with horror. Was this all that was left of some poor unfortunate creature struck down by a bomb? Fortunately not. As the shaken cyclist suddenly realized, it was simply the remains of a beetroot patch.

And some people's reactions were, to say the least, bizarre. The veteran BBC radio commentator, Frank Gillard, wandering half dazed through the inferno, came across a woman already sweeping up glass from the pavement, singing at the top of her voice, as if she didn't have a care in the world.

But now it was almost over. For the loss of five planes, Exeter had been gravely hurt. Despite official optimism and newspaper reports next day about "undamaged morale", the heart of Exeter had been burnt out. The principal shopping centre was in ruins. Most of the essential services—gas, water, electricity, sewage—had been knocked out. Some 1,500 buildings were destroyed and nearly 2,700 severely damaged. And, in just one week, the old Cathedral city had lost nearly a thousand of its citizens dead or wounded.

That Monday Mr Morrison, the Home Secretary, told the annual conference of the United Textile Factory Workers in far-off Blackpool, which was yet to have a single German bomb drop on it, "I want justice for the German people. I am against that foolish and purposeless vindicativeness which was set up and imposed on the German people after the last war."[25]

The reaction of his audience of trade unionists is not recorded, but Morrison's sentiments were certainly not shared by Air Marshal Harris. That same day, in an interview with the London editor of the Australian *Sydney Sun*, Harris made this forthright announcement:

> We are going to bomb Germany incessantly, and I have no doubt that the day is coming when the United States and ourselves between us will put such a force in the air that the Germans will scream for mercy. . . . If I could send up 20,000 bombers to Germany tonight, Germany would not be in the war tomorrow.[26]

Soon, very soon, Harris would be on his way to achieving at least part of that aim.

THREE

In May, 1942, Winston Churchill had been his King's First Minister for two years. It had been a period of defeat after defeat. The Japanese had seized the whole of Britain's Eastern Empire with the exception of India. Britain had been run out of the Continent. Germany dominated the Mediterranean and even now, Egypt, the last bastion west of the Suez Canal, was under threat. As for the nation itself, it was near starvation. Admiral Doenitz's wolf packs in the Atlantic were monthly sinking thousands of tons of shipping bringing food to Britain. It seemed that May as if Germany was winning the Battle of the Atlantic.

Indeed, in a month's time there would be a concerted effort to get rid of the Old Man by a vote of no-confidence in the Commons. In the end, Churchill would win the support of both sides of the House and receive a tremendous ovation. But on 10 May, 1942, Churchill felt that he had to give account to the nation of his two years in office. In spite of his approaching seventies, he was vigorous, jaunty and forthright as he spoke over the wireless that Sunday evening, one week after the second Baedeker raid on Exeter.

There had been "many misfortunes and disappointments", he admitted, but after those reverses the country was now moving towards "complete and final victory". Then, scornfully referring to "Herr Hitler's" threats, he went on:

> He [Hitler] warns us solemnly that if we go on smashing up the German cities, his war factories and his bases, he will retaliate against our cathedrals and historic monuments—if they are not too far inland. We have heard his threats before. Eighteen months ago, in September, 1940, when he thought he had an

overwhelming air force at his command, he declared that he would rub out—that was the actual expression, *rub out!*—our towns and cities. And he certainly had a good try. Now the boot is on the other foot.

We have a long list of German cities in which all the vital industries of the German war machine are established. All these it will be our stern duty to deal with, as we have already dealt with Lübeck and Rostock and half a dozen important places. The civil population of Germany have, however, an easy way to escape from these severities. All they have to do is to leave the cities where munition work is being carried on—abandon their work and go out into the fields and watch their home fires burning from a distance.[1]

Churchill's declaration was in full accord with Harris's own strategy and plans. Now the Old Man ended on a note of hope.

Therefore tonight I give you a message of good cheer. You deserve it and the facts endorse it. But be it good or be it bad cheer, it will make no difference to us. We shall drive on to the end and do our duty, win or die. God helping us, we can do no other.[2]

Even James Lansdale Hodson, who thought that "Winston needs reminding once a month that he isn't God", called the speech "magnificent" for Churchill had used "language the enemy will understand".[3]

It was indeed a timely speech. The nation was weary of the war. There had been too many defeats and too many shortages. Apart from the Baedeker raids there was not much to spur the ordinary folk into defiance. Victories were non-existent and, although no one was actually starving, the national diet had been reduced to a drab starchy minimum. By contrast, over in Germany there were no problems for the average working-class mother buying her full allocation of butter, beef and the like. In three years' time the first British troops to invade the Reich would be amazed at how ruddy-cheeked and well-fed the people looked, and how well their cellars were stocked with food. Even Montgomery remarked that the tales he had heard throughout the war of the Germans starving were all "bunkum".

In Britain, on the other hand, most people were wan and pasty-faced, yawning all the time from chronic exhaustion and undernourishment. Investigating the mood in the northern industrial cities that May, Hodson noted among the workers a sense of detachment from the war. "All the men care about is the wage packet," one manager told him, while another complained that some of the younger workers "seemed to think they would be no worse off under Hitler". Hodson also found that, even in wartime, industry was still plagued by the trade unions' lines of demarcation. As the superintendent of a naval dockyard told him, "We're too old-fashioned. We've got lines of demarcation they had when they built wooden ships!" But a workman objected to the diarist, "What about apprenticeship? If a lad had served five years in a trade he isn't going to let Tom, Dick and Harry do his job."[4]

For two years Churchill had bullied, cajoled, inspired his war-weary nation, trying to give it a sense of mission, forcing it, against all the objections and complaints from high and low, to believe that one day Britain really would triumph against Hitler's Reich. But the Old Man knew he had to give his people a victory, any kind of victory, to inspire them to fight on during the dark months ahead—and also to restore their waning faith in his own leadership.

Despite pressure from both Moscow and Washington, Churchill refused to commit the Army in Britain to any invasion of France this summer. From the Army's showing in other theatres of war, he had no confidence in its ability to win on the beaches of the Continent. "When will they ever fight?" he had complained in despair. For in those days he was all too often afflicted by his "black dog", as he called his moods of depression. Even the Eighth Army in Egypt was on the run again, having "lost a battle which they felt they ought to have won", in the words of Colonel Jacob at Auchinleck's Eighth Army HQ. "The discipline of the Army is no longer what it used to be," Jacob went on. "The aims set before people are negative . . . and it still does not seem to have been brought home to people that it was a war for their own existence."[5]

And so it was that Churchill turned to his abrasive, no-nonsense Air Marshal Harris; he alone could provide hope of victory in these dark days of May, 1942. And Harris was not a man to turn down an opportunity.

On Sunday, 4 May, the night that Exeter was bombed, Harris had gone to dine with Churchill at Chequers. With him he bore a magical number; at least he regarded it as magical. Up to now the maximum force sent against a single target had been 228 RAF bombers; indeed, the official front-line strength of Bomber Command was only 350. But for days now, ever since the fourth raid on Rostock, Harris's staff had been working on ways and means of increasing that figure. This was why Cheshire and a score of other training and conversion squadron commanders had been asked for everything they could raise in the way of additional strength. Even Coastal Command had been consulted. Now the magical figure that Harris had striven for had been achieved: Bomber Command would be able to muster the unprecedented number of 1,000 bombers for a single raid!

Thus, after a heavy dinner, Harris had broached his great plan. He wished to bomb a German target with this massive strike force and was prepared to lose one tenth of the force in the undertaking. Churchill had warmed to the plan immediately. Instinct told him that it might well bring the victory he needed to restore the nation's flagging spirits. So, without much discussion, he gave Harris his approval. Later Harris wrote:

> As I drove home from there in my Bentley at three a.m.—it was only ten minutes from my home at Springfield—I found myself humming *Malbrouck s'en va t'en guerre* ["Marlborough is going to war"] . . . This tune always came into my head whenever I had just left him. The spirit of Marlborough did indeed breathe in his descendant and, most emphatically, he was going to war.[6]

Harris gave his plan the code-name "Millennium", a code-name that had been originally earmarked for the start of the Second Front (it had to do much later with Overlord). But there were plenty of problems still to be overcome for this great 1,000 bomber raid on an as yet unknown German target. As Harris knew,

> The dangers were many and varied. If anything went seriously wrong . . . then I should be committing not only the whole of my front-line strength but absolutely all my reserve in a single battle. Our whole programme of training and expansion might conceivably be wrecked . . . [but] the result of using an adequate bomber force against Germany would be there for all the world to see and I should be able to press for the aircraft, crews and equipment we needed with far more effect than by putting forward theoretic arguments.[7]

It was blatant empire-building; but what did it matter, Churchill must have reasoned, as long as it helped to bring final victory.

During the weeks that followed there were no further German raids on Baedeker targets, only a spate of tip-and-run attacks on 23 May. The raiders swept in from the Channel and dropped bombs on a stretch of coast from Deal to Dawlish before roaring away unharmed; for, despite all Pile's efforts, he only managed to borrow 28 light anti-aircraft guns from inland to defend an area needing six times that number. Meanwhile, profiting from the lack of action, Harris's staff officers laboured to reach the magical figure of 1,000 bombers.

The Admiralty refused to allow Coastal Command to loan the hundred or so planes it had promised for the great operation. Flying Training Command had promised to contribute twenty-one Wellingtons, but in the end they produced a mere four. More pressure was put on the Operational Training Groups. There was a whole-scale levee of not only trainees, but instructors too. Cheshire himself was to fly with a crew of trainee sergeants, although he had just been taken off "ops". By the time all sources had been tapped, Numbers 91 and 92 Operational Training Groups had provided 369 aircraft, some manned by instructors, while the Heavy Conversion Units, to which Cheshire belonged, fielded every last Stirling, Halifax and Lancaster that could possibly fly.

On 23 May the preliminary orders went out to alert the fifty-two airfields selected for the attack. Normal operations were virtually suspended. Two days later crews and bombers started to move to the new fields. Tension began to mount. On the 26th Bomber Command HQ issued the final operation order, which opened with a rousing preamble:

> The stage of the war has been reached when the morale of the German people is likely to be seriously affected by an unprecedented blow of great magnitude in the West. . . . We are in a position to deliver this blow from the air. . . . Apart from the effect on morale of such an attack, the unprecedented damage which will be caused is bound to have a considerable effect on the issue of the war. . . . If every unit conscientiously plays its part . . . it is estimated that a force of 1,081 bombers can be employed in . . . the greatest air attack of all time.[8]

So now the aircrews knew what they'd only suspected so far. The only question that remained was—what was the target going to be?

On the morning of Saturday, 30 May, Harris made his decision. He had several choices of target, but as he walked from his house to

Bomber Command HQ that morning he decided on the one which his crews would attack this night.

Unlike so many wartime headquarters, this one was purpose-built and new, opened in 1940. It was so well hidden, seventy-five feet underground, among the dripping beechwoods near the village of Walters Ash, that the Luftwaffe never did locate it. Harris himself lived close by and usually walked over to "the Hole", as it was inevitably called, to attend the morning briefing sessions, known just as inevitably as "morning prayers".

As he strode towards the headquarters, the weather must have played a role in his considerations. The air was heavy with rain and dark clouds scudded across the sky above him. Bad weather was no great problem in the usual sort of raid, but to launch 1,000 bombers into this cloud might well be courting disaster. It was not just the risk of collision which worried Harris as he approached the guarded entrance to the Hole. He was also concerned about the risks involved in landing shot-up aircraft, piloted by weary crews, after the raid. There were always more crashes on landing than after taking off.

But Harris knew he couldn't risk delaying the operation much longer. He had many enemies at court. Sooner or later they would persuade Churchill to break up the 1,000-bomber force for employment elsewhere.

At ten minutes past nine Harris walked into the high-ceilinged operations room. The hum of voices died almost immediately. Although his staff were devoted to him, they were also afraid of his sharp tongue, for the Air Marshal did not tolerate fools gladly and he had no time at all for what he called contemptuously "young Jacks-in-office". At the front of the big room sat the group-captains, responsible for operations and intelligence, the Army liaison colonel, the Navy liaison captain, and a host of other top brass. But this damp morning it was the Meteorological Officer, Magnus Spence, whom Harris had come to hear.

Spence delivered his forecast in an emotionless voice. The forecast wasn't good. There would be storms and heavy cloud over northern Germany. Harris's face hardened. Then came a glimmer of hope as Spence said, "In the south cloud formations could break up." Harris flashed a quick look at Saundby, his trusted deputy, and the latter smiled as Spence continued: "There is a fifty-fifty chance that the cloud will clear from the Cologne area by midnight. The home base will, on the whole, be clear of cloud."[9]

Spence finished and waited. Everyone was looking at Harris. The decision was his. He had already chosen the target, unknown to his staff, but there was still the question of the weather. Would it hold long enough for 1,000 bombers to clobber their target within the ninety minutes allowed for the operation?

Harris's face revealed nothing. He stood there saying nothing, staring at the map of Europe. Dudley Saward, his chief radar officer, who was in the Hole that Saturday morning, later described the scene in graphic detail:

> Slowly his forefinger moved across the Continent of Europe and came to rest on a town in Germany. The pressure of his finger bent back the end of the joint and drove the blood from the top of his finger nail, leaving a half circle of white. He turned to his Senior Air Staff Officer, his face still expressionless. "The Thousand Plan tonight!"[10]

His finger was resting on Germany's fourth largest city, Cologne.

All over North-Eastern England the aircrews were preparing for the assault to come, as the damp mist curled in and out of the dripping hangars and Nissen huts. At RAF Croft, a muddy Yorkshire airfield known to its crews as "Sinking-in-the-Ouse", one newcomer, Irish-born Sergeant A. Mitchell, was amazed at how casual everyone was in spite of the fact that they all knew something was "on" this night.

> Later, I found out this was all a front. But that morning, I was amazed at the way they could eat their "wads" and drink their coffee, chatting away as if this was just another day. There were even fellows still "crewing up", casually asking other blokes if they'd found a plane or a skipper yet. It wasn't at all what I thought an op should be like, especially one like this which was going to involve a thousand "kites" for the very first time.[11]

Gradually the crews started to head for the locker rooms where they would change into their flying gear. Mitchell spotted a notice on one door which read "LEAVE YOUR LOCKER KEYS WITH THE NCO/i/c LOCKER ROOM". He wondered why, but as a new boy he didn't dare to ask. Later he would learn that the keys would be needed for the RAF police and chaplain to collect a man's personal effects if he didn't come back. This night, some 600 out of 6,000 of these young men wouldn't come back.

For ten shillings a day they were flying to their death, while fifty

110

miles from RAF Croft, eighteen-year-old Durham miners were going on strike for another two shillings and sixpence to add to the nine and eightpence they were already getting per shift. After three days out, they would receive the extra money. By then sorrowing families throughout the country would be receiving the telegram that began "The Air Ministry regrets . . ."

Now the crews began to go through their pre-flight ritual, for already most of these young men had developed an almost primeval faith in lucky charms and superstition. One man always played the first strains of the Warsaw Concerto just before setting off for his bomber. Another insisted on urinating on his aircraft. Many took with them a lucky teddy bear, a lucky rabbit's foot, or if they were Catholic, lucky medals pinned to their vests, all "blessed personally by the Pope in Rome". Some prayed before take-off, but not many.

Slowly darkness began to sweep across the fields of Yorkshire and East Anglia. The crews tucked into the last ritual meal of bacon and eggs—those who were not nauseated with fear at the prospect of what was to come. Then they were mustered, calling out their names as they were ticked off on the roster. Clumsy in their thick fur flying gear, lugging their parachutes with them, they struggled into the waiting "fifteen hundreds" to be taken to where the silent metal birds waited for them.

Up in the control tower, the staff officers tensed, as the phones jingled and messengers came and went, clattering up and down the steel ladder outside. On the field engine after engine burst into life after a series of asthmatic grunts. Scarlet exhaust flames stabbed the darkness. The night air was filled with the stench of petrol. Zero hour was approaching fast.

Security for the great raid had been lousy. One WAAF clerk was confined to barracks because she had taken down the whole operational order, including the name of the target, Cologne, *in clear!* Some clot, as her CO told her, "ought to be shot".

Mrs Elizabeth Stebbing, who worked at RAF Scampton, was horrified when she joined a bus queue after work that rainy Saturday afternoon. Standing next to her a total stranger opened the conversation with the words, "I hear you are sending a thousand bombers to Cologne tonight . . . "[12]

Even today writer Michael Bowyer can vividly recall how his father was "most upset on that Saturday when we discovered through someone's indiscretion that 1,000 bombers were about to destroy Cologne that very night".[13]

On a little railway bridge not far from the bomber station at Linton-on-Ouse, a young woman bumped into an RAF mechanic "who excused his clumsiness because he had been working on the bombers which were going to attack Cologne that night". Many years later she still wondered how an "ordinary erk" could have known "something as secret and as important as that".[14]

That lady and all the others who already knew the secret of the first 1,000-bomber raid would have been even more surprised if they had known that Saturday that the great plan seemed to be known in Germany too. Forty-odd years later, former opera star Erika Wagner recalled her experiences that day in Cologne.

> During the war I was engaged in the *Fronttheater* [a sort of German ENSA]. I often gave popular song recitals to the soldiers both in the Reich and abroad. Once, I had even given a concert in Russia where the price of admission was one log of wood—to heat the stove which warmed the makeshift theatre. Anyway, on that Saturday I was booked to entertain the garrison at the local barracks out in the suburbs of Cologne. That afternoon, however, I received a phone call from the camp commander himself. He warned me not to come and to cancel the concert, for there was "going to be a big raid on Cologne that night". I cancelled, of course, but I didn't take him seriously. How could he know, I asked myself at the time.[15]

How indeed. We don't know. All we do know is that his suggestion to Frau Wagner probably saved her life. The barracks was hit that night, with the bomb exploding directly in the camp theatre.

At exactly half past eleven that Saturday night the first two-engined Stirling bomber took its place at the end of the mile-long runway at RAF Wyton. At the controls Wing-Commander Macdonald waited for the signal to start moving. To the front a green light flickered. Over the intercom came the metallic voice of his bomb-aimer, "You've got your green, skipper—take her away!" The Stirling started to roll forward.

Almost simultaneously, other Stirlings, Manchesters, Wellingtons, Halifaxes began to roll down runways at fifty-two airfields throughout the north-east. Throttle levers were jerked open. Engines roared to full pitch. Brakes were unlocked, and then, as the engines shrieked in protest, the heavily laden bombers were airborne, disappearing into the gloom.

112

Outside the airfields many people watched them go and wondered at their number, as Feltwell postman Peter Greenham remembers:

> There were bombers in every quarter of the sky . . . from Alconbury, Wyton, Oakington, Mildenhall, Honington, Lakenheath, everywhere. The sound of their engines was like a great waterfall. It was frightening enough for us. God knows what it must have been like for those poor devils in Cologne.[16]

Now they began to form into groups above the North Sea. They would attack in three waves, led by the Wellingtons of No 3 Group, which carried with it a very high-ranking passenger indeed: no less a person than Air Vice-Marshal "Jackie" Baldwin, who had virtually smuggled himself aboard one of his own aircraft. Harris had strictly forbidden his senior officers to fly, possibly because of security, but Baldwin was not going to be left out of this particular show. Let other officers stand on the tarmac and salute their crews as they went to do battle; he was going to fight with his chaps.

Although there was some icing and cloud over the North Sea, weather conditions were improving rapidly. All the same, Pilot Harry Langton from RAF Honington was worried about the weather. He and the other Wellingtons from his station were in the van of the great attack. They were the "Guy Fawkes boys" charged with dropping the incendiaries that would light up the target for the less experienced crews behind them. But what if a sudden thunderstorm and heavy rain obscured the fires; would the rest still be able to bomb accurately?

Langton need not have worried. The weather would be perfect for their task. Soon Cheshire and his crew of trainee sergeants would see, as they crossed the Dutch coast, "an angry beacon on the moonlit horizon". That angry beacon was the blazing city of Cologne, 150 miles away.

FOUR

So far Cologne had had a good war. Of course, it had been raided before. Indeed, Cheshire had won the first of his three DSOs for having brought back a Wellington with a ten-foot hole in it from a raid on the city in 1940. But up till now the British bombing had been the merest pin-prick. It had in no way affected the life of the city, famed for its Rhenish *Frohsinn* or *joie de vivre* which found its ultimate expression in the Lenten carnival, when for three days the wine flowed, wedding rings were discreetly hidden and anything went.

The local authorities were more concerned about the British leaflet raids than the bombing ones. Whenever the RAF dropped leaflets the Hitler Youth was ordered out into the streets "to collect them *unread*", as the then fifteen-year-old Willi Niessen, a secret collector of this forbidden literature, remembered many years later. "Tommy propaganda was thought more dangerous than their bombs."[1]

Thus it was that, as the sirens started to shrill their warning at thirty-eight minutes after midnight, there was no panic-stricken rush for the shelters, those built into the city's stout cellars or the overground ones, which sometimes were seven storeys high and carried a flak gun mounted on the roof.[2] Even Erika Wagner, who had been warned of what was to come, took her time. She had heard both the siren and the warning broadcast on the wireless when a bomber force approached a German city. Even when the announcer cried excitedly, *"The target is Cologne. . . . The target is Cologne!"* she still took her time.

It was only when her dog began to howl that she decided to go to the outside shelter. She was just in time. She heard a shriek like a

114

railway train belting full-out through a station, followed an instant later by a tremendous explosion. The blast lifted her right off her feet and flung her into the bunker. There she lay for a few moments, gasping for breath, while outside the bombs began to rain down in crazy profusion and Cologne started to burn.

As the first wave swamped the target with their HE and incendiaries, the second-wave crews now approaching the German frontier could hardly believe the evidence of their own eyes. Some thought the huge blaze on the horizon was a dummy inferno created by the defenders to confuse them. Others believed it was a forest fire. In their surprise they did not even notice the heavy flak coming up from München-Gladbach.

But as they came closer they could see that the huge fires were coming from Cologne, dwarfing the flickering of searchlights and the stab of flak. Even at that height they could see that the city's defences were being swamped. The searchlights wandered erratically around the burning sky like torches held by drunks. The flak was fading away, too, as the 88mm gunners began to run out of ammunition and no trucks bringing fresh supplies could get across the blocked river bridges. Soon over 600 square acres of the city was ablaze with so many fires that bewildered bomb-aimers simply did not know what to aim for. As pilot Rupert Oakley remembers: "The whole area seemed ablaze with fires and my navigator wasn't quite sure where to bomb. I said, 'Well, start a bloody fire somewhere . . . where it's not burning!' "[3]

Pilot "Micky" Martin was so awed by the conflagration below that, despite the danger, he circled the city three times before dropping his bombs. He had never seen anything like it before. "New boy" Sergeant Mitchell experienced the same sense of awe. "In the years to come I'd see plenty of fires like those at Cologne that night, but I never forget that first one. It's in my mind to this day, I can tell you."[4]

Down below the civilians crouched in their shelters, while the lights flickered and threatened to go out with every new explosion, quailing before that awful cacophony of noise: the massive drone of hundreds of engines, the sharp crack and thwack of flak guns, the piercing whistle of falling bombs, followed an instant later by earth-shattering explosions.

Now and then a vicious tongue of flame would penetrate a crack in the walls or lick through the side of the iron shelter doors, throwing everything into stark relief for a fleeting second, giving the terrified occupants a brief picture of themselves as they huddled, hands clapped to ears, eyes wide with fear. Once in such an instant, Frau Wagner glimpsed outside and saw to her horror that incendiaries were burning and dropping all around her house. Without thinking, she stumbled to her feet and fought her way outside, pelting across the debris-littered street.

Fires blazed everywhere. Masonry slithered down in dusty avalanches. Apartment houses swayed and trembled like theatre backdrops. Racing into her house and upstairs to the attic, she started to fling buckets of sand on the burning incendiaries, and when the sand gave out she beat at the flames with a long-handled shovel. Only when she was satisfied that the flames were out did she return to the safety of the shelter.

Young Willi Niessen, the secret leaflet collector, was another who left his shelter on an irrational impulse that night. He had caught a glimpse of incendiaries dropping and bursting into flame on the roof opposite. He dashed outside into a world gone crazy. He reasoned that if the fire-bombs had dropped on the other side of the roof they would have dropped on his family's house too.

He was right. There were flames coming from the attic. With another youth, he pelted upstairs. Normally rather indecisive— indeed he was destined for a legal office—he grabbed a shovel and tackled the bomb. Within minutes he and the other boy had removed the danger. For a few moments they stood staring at the terrible scenes around them as the whole of southern Cologne burned furiously. Then they became aware of their danger once more and fled downstairs to the street.

Outside they were met by a deafening scream of motors. A four-engined bomber was coming down the Geldorpstrasse at little more than roof-top height, machine guns chattering, spraying the area with white tracer.

Gauleiter Grohé, the unpopular political head of the Cologne area who was assassinated by a Russian slave labourer towards the end of the war, later confessed in a letter to Party Secretary Bormann that the city's civil defence had virtually broken down during the attack. There had simply been too many explosions and fires. Even so, the hard-pressed firemen and wardens—not volunteers, as in Britain, but conscripts—fought back the best they could.

Cologne was an inland port, with a large trade in merchandise brought in along the Rhine by barge from Holland, France,

116

Switzerland and the like. As a result, the local firemen were forced to fight fires ranging from synthetic rubber to molasses. There were huge, almost unstoppable blazes with treacle pouring down the cobbled street like molten lava. Time and again, desperate firemen, fighting to the last, were cut off by the flames.

One horrified woman, blundering from street to street, trying to find refuge from the ever-advancing flames tearing down the alleyways of the *Altstadt* like a blow-torch, came across a fire-engine, its motor still running, complete with crew.

> At first they looked alive to me, except that they were naked save for their helmets and boots. Then I saw they were dead and slowly being tanned a sickly yellow by the heat from a building blazing nearby. I never did find out what had happened to them. Perhaps a shock wave had collapsed their lungs or something. But they were dead all right, each man in his place, sitting upright, with the motor still ticking patiently away.[5]

Similarly nightmarish scenes took place all over Cologne that night, etching themselves for ever on the minds of those who saw them. The naked woman running past the Cathedral with her hair on fire; the mother crumpled dead in a gutter, dead child clutched to her bosom; the air-raid warden tripping over a jackboot with a soldier's leg in it—and nothing else left of the body; the crazed brewery horse galloping down the street, mane on fire; the old man gathering what was left of his wife in an enamel washing-up pail ... this night in Cologne everyone was finding out the bitter truth of Goebbels's statement that *"We're all in the front line now!"*

But still the RAF bomber crews rained down their bombs, adding to the inferno below. In the end *Gauleiter* Grohé reported that there were 12,000 fires in all, of which 2,500 were major outbreaks. All public services had broken down. There was no water, gas or electricity and no telephones. All forms of transport save trucks had ceased, with most of the tramsheds and trams—the city's major form of public transport—knocked out. Lord Cherwell's ruthless "de-housing" policy was paying off, with a record 45,000 people being made homeless, though for the size of the raid the death roll was modest: 468 civilians killed and another 5,000-odd injured.

And still the bombs dropped, one every six seconds. Down below it was light enough to read a newspaper by the glow of the fires and the spluttering incendiaries. Desperate men and women fought the flames, but all too often in vain. Fireman Walther Seidel remembers to this day the cloying stench of burnt flesh as he doubled into a local home for the elderly. There he found senile, terrified old women, with their clothes and hair ablaze, groping their way through the thick white smoke. "Pushing, shouting and heaving", Seidel propelled them out to the street—but conditions were not much better outside.

> Incendiary bombs were spurting white flames and setting fire to the tar on the road. Mothers with children rushed blindly by the fire bombs. Some blazing wood fell on one little girl and set her dress alight. An old man flung himself on top of her, using his coat and hands to douse the flames which rose straight up to her hair. Somehow I herded the old ladies towards a small green patch near a square—a cemetery.[6]

There, with a grim amusement, Seidel watched the old women lie down on the tombs as if already dead, like corpses waiting for burial.

Many citizens of Cologne that night fled to the surrounding countryside, the green belt created by a former burgomaster of Cologne, Dr Adenauer, the future Chancellor of post-war Germany. But there was no respite even in the woods.

Karl Schmidt and his wife Gaby were following a small track into the woods when he tripped:

> I fell over a shattered tree and then stopped. In the pale light of the moon and fires that filtered through the trees I could see in a small clearing an awful sight. Ghastly! The place was strewn with bodies—glimmering where the strange light caught the whiteness of their skin. There were children lying higgledy-piggledy across each other, large corpses flung about in grotesque positions, some limbless, one near me had no head. My wife's hand slipped from mine as she slumped in a faint to the soft earth.
>
> I felt empty and sick. I, too, sank down with my back against a tree stump, cradling my wife. All those people with the same idea, thinking they were safe and now lying cold and wet among the rotting leaves.
>
> Above and around us was a terrible roaring and crashing—engines, guns, bright flashes and blasts that shook the ground. Bombs were dropping everywhere. I thought we, too, would soon be dead, dead as those already lying there.
>
> We began to pray.[7]

But at last the terrible raid was over. Gradually people realized the bombers had gone and they began to leave their shelters. In the streets of Lindenthal, a suburb of Cologne, one woman was appalled by "the rubble that had once been the beautiful houses of our neighbours. And yet there was among the people who stood in those streets at first an elation, a kind of wild joy—we had survived!"[8]

Later soldiers came clambering over the rubble, prodding it with metal rods, on the look-out for survivors. With them came a steady trickle of civilian refugees from the city centre, who told the people of Lindenthal that central Cologne was "a mass of ruins". One of that group was film-maker Gerhard Steinborn. It was his task during raids to make the official film for Goebbels' Ministry. Now, his face and hair white with dust, he collapsed in his wife's arms and sobbed broken-heartedly, "Cologne has disappeared!"

But his wife had hardened her heart to fear and suffering, even as her husband lay sobbing in her arms. Later she would swear, "Never before that night had I known such terror, but I know one thing now—I shall never be afraid again."[9]

Bomb as he might, Harris would never break the spirit of such people.

Reichsmarschall Hermann Goering received his high-ranking visitors at his castle at Veldenstein in Franconia, the castle he had inherited from the wealthy long-time Jewish lover of his now dead mother. He was wearing a uniform of his own design: a dove-grey tunic with broad white silk lapels over breeches and red Russian leather boots. As always his chest was covered with glittering decorations.

After greeting his visitors—Milch, the half-Jewish Inspector of the Luftwaffe ("*I* decide who's a Jew here!" Goering had snorted when told of Milch's ancestry), and Albert Speer, the clever young Minister of Armaments—Goering squeezed his vast backside between the armrests of his huge chair and listened once again to the reports coming in from Cologne.

Speer, who knew him well, could see that the *Reichsmarschall* was getting worked up. His eyes, which always looked too small for that vast expanse of face, were starting to glitter. Suddenly he opened his mouth and filled the room with a stentorian bellow. "*Impossible!*" he cried at his elegant adjutant. "That many bombs cannot be dropped in a single night. Connect me with the *Gauleiter* of Cologne!"[10]

Grohé was brought to the telephone in Cologne and immediately Goering set about him. Back in 1940 Goering had boasted that never a bomb would drop on Germany. Now it appeared that over

1,000 planes had dropped a huge tonnage on Cologne; he wouldn't have it. His reputation was at stake. "The report from your police commissioner is a stinking lie!" he bellowed over the phone. "I tell you as *Reichsmarschall* that the figures cited are simply too high. How can you dare to report such fantasies to the Führer?"

Grohé started to explain but Goering interrupted. Grohé's estimates were wrong, he said, insisting again that it wasn't possible so many bombs could have been dropped in a single raid. Shouting and screaming into the phone, he ordered Grohé to change his figures. How could he, *Reichsmarschall* Goering, be wrong?

He slammed the phone down. Then, to his visitors' astonishment, as if nothing had happened Goering gave them a guided tour of the castle:

> As if this were most serene peacetime, he had blueprints
> brought in and explained to us what a magnificent citadel he
> would be building to replace the simple Biedermeier house of
> his parents in the courtyard of the old ruins. But first of all he
> wanted a reliable air-raid shelter built. The plans for that were
> already drawn up.[11]

Goering was not the only one trying to stick his head in the sand that day. As Minister of Propaganda, Goebbels was ready enough to play up the damage and casualties caused by this "extermination raid", but he wildly distorted the number of British planes involved. According to the first German broadcast in English that Monday morning, while a shattered Cologne tried to pick up the pieces, "The number of British planes operating in the district of Cologne itself did not exceed seventy."[12]

In Britain they could afford to ignore Goebbels' lies, for they already knew from aerial reconnaissance and the pilots' debriefing reports the vast amount of damage that Cologne had suffered in the first 1,000-bomber raid. A jubilant Harris rang up Churchill, who had just flown in from Washington after a trip to see Roosevelt. "I told him that the operation had been successful and that only thirty-nine aircraft were missing, one less than my estimate of forty," Harris said later, commenting happily on Churchill's satisfaction with the news. Best of all, he went on, "Churchill now knew that we had an immensely powerful weapon which would give us that initiative that only comes from taking the offensive. . . . No one understood better than he the vast strategic consequences of this single operation which proved that a serious bombing offensive against Germany itself was a real possibility."[13]

Churchill was indeed delighted. He sent Harris the following telegram:

> I congratulate you and the whole of Bomber Command upon the remarkable feat of organization which enabled you to despatch over a thousand bombers to the Cologne area in a single night and without confusion to concentrate their action over the target in so short a time as one hour and a half. This proof of the growing power of the British bomber force is also the herald of what Germany will receive, city by city, from now on.[14]

The Ministry of Information immediately set about preparing a pamphlet which read: "Ninety minutes' bombing created devastation over an area eight times the size of the City of London. . . . Steadily the storm will increase in violence."[15] The same tenor was taken by the newspapers, which crowed that the Germans were now going to be squeezed "till the pips squeak". This gleeful attitude was shared by the vast majority of civilians. Germany had had her own way for too long; it was time the tables were turned.

But there were some in Britain who objected to the indiscriminate bombing in Cologne, however many factories had been hit by the bombs, and who detested the public gloating over the miseries and sufferings of fellow human beings. Secret government surveys revealed that "Nothing has given such a lift to public opinion for many months as the raid on Cologne." However, as the reports went on, "Some regret has been expressed, particularly by older people, that women and children should have to suffer from our bombing: but not one has been heard to suggest that we should limit our attacks on this account." And so, concluded the reports, most people felt it was "the only way, however distasteful, to drive home to the German people what their airmen have been doing in other countries".[16]

Indeed, those who openly deplored what was happening over Germany were few in number, a handful of churchmen and the like. The great majority approved of this new terror warfare and were overjoyed by the news of the huge bomber raid on Cologne—as was one particular visitor to London that Monday.

General "Hap" Arnold was the four-star commander of the American Army Air Corps. He was thrilled by this massive air attack, the first of its kind in history. He declared to the pressmen interviewing him that day that it was "a wonderful exhibition" and he was looking forward to the time when it would be possible to make raids like that every night, until the enemy could no longer survive.

Then he added a few words that would soon ring all too true for the young men of the US Eighth Air Force, now beginning to arrive in East Anglia to take their part in the war against Germany: "Our enemies have demonstrated that they are willing to take their losses. *We must be willing to take our losses, too.*"[17]

Meanwhile, back in Germany the sirens over Cologne were sounding yet again. Willi Niessen, out among the smouldering ruins, glanced up at the sky and saw three silver shapes, high above the brown puffballs of flak. They were the latest British aircraft, the Mosquito. What was going on?

A few seconds later he found out. Leaflets came tumbling down in profusion. The Tommies weren't dropping bombs this time, but paper! Willi grabbed a leaflet and stuffed it into his pocket (he still has it to this day). Later at home he read the message printed on both sides in red. It was short and simple in its brutality: *"Die Offensive der Royal Air Force in ihrer neuen Form hat begonnen!"*

"The RAF's offensive in its new form has commenced": this was the problem occupying the minds of many of the Nazi leaders that Monday. Goering, as we have seen, would not believe the figures given to him by Grohé. Speer snorted that the RAF couldn't keep it up. General Jeschonnek, Goering's long suffering Chief-of-Staff who would soon commit suicide because he was unable to defend the Reich, echoed Goering's line when he met the Führer that day. His hands trembled visibly as he prepared to make his statement about Cologne. "According to preliminary reports," he told Hitler, "we estimate that two hundred enemy aircraft have penetrated our defences. The damage is heavy . . . we are still waiting for final estimates."

Hitler exploded with rage. "You are still waiting for final estimates?" he yelled. "And the Luftwaffe thinks there were only two hundred aircraft?" His pasty face contorted with scorn. "The Luftwaffe was probably asleep last night! . . . But I was not asleep. I stay awake when one of my cities is under fire. And I thank the Almighty that I can rely on my *Gauleiter*, even if the Luftwaffe deceives me. Let me tell you what *Gauleiter* Grohé has to say." He glared at an ashen-faced Jeschonnek. "There were a thousand or more English aircraft! Do you hear? A thousand, perhaps twelve hundred! . . . Maybe more!"[18]

Later, when Goering arrived, Hitler pointedly ignored him. He refused to take the hand of the man who had once been regarded as his successor. Instead he upbraided him in front of junior officers.

Goering, swaying between protestation and panic, stammered that he wanted to increase the production of fighters. Hitler would not listen. He ranted that he wasn't interested in defence, he wanted *revenge*! Goering said he would do his best, but Hitler was not listening any more.

That night the second most popular voice in Britain—after Churchill's—began to speak on his regular 9.30 wireless broadcast; millions of people tuned in to hear him, even though they detested him. For the voice was that of "Lord Haw-Haw", the Irish renegade William Joyce, whom the British would hang one day. "Mr Churchill boasts of the attack on Cologne as an instalment of the hell that Germany is to receive," he snarled in that slow arrogant manner of his. "The German attitude is, 'Give us more hell—as much as you can—and we shall repay that hell *with interest*!' "[19]

FIVE

All that Monday, 1 June, 1942, the media regaled the nation with titbits of new information about the great raid. "OVER 1,000 BOMBERS RAID COLOGNE," proclaimed *The Times*, "Biggest Air Attack of the War: 2,000 Tons of Bombs in 40 Minutes." The listening public were treated to an eyewitness account of the raid from a South African bomb-aimer—for the attack force had contained men from every dominion (as well as three Americans from the "Royal Texas Air Force", as they nicknamed themselves):

> The flames were higher than I had ever seen before. The buildings were skeletons in the midst of fires. The blast of the bombs was hurling walls themselves across the flames. As we came away we saw more and more of our aircraft below us silhouetted against the flames. I identified Wellingtons, Halifaxes, Manchesters and other Lancasters, lit by the light of the moon. They were doing exactly as we did, going in according to plan, coming out according to plan, and making their way home.[1]

It was all good stirring stuff and the "Brylcreem Boys", as the Army called the RAF, were well and truly the heroes of the day.

Years later Harris wrote of that day that he believed it had been the turning point of the war in the air. "The dominating offensive weapon of the war was at last being used. . . . My own opinion is that we should never have had a real bomber offensive if it had not been for the thousand-bomber raid on Cologne."[2] And this night he was going to launch another huge raid. Tonight the target would be Essen.

*

Undoubtedly that Monday the 20,000-odd citizens of Britain's most famed tourist city, Canterbury, enjoyed the discomfiture of Cologne. "I remember well," one of them recalled many years later, "listening to Alvar Lidell telling us about the raid on the one o'clock news and thinking to myself: By God, this time old Jerry has really caught a packet! And about time too after what he had done to Kent for the last couple of years."[3]

For ever since May, 1940, the county of Kent had really been in the front line. Since the fall of France, Dover had endured constant shellfire from the French coast, so close that on a clear day British officers could read the time on the station clock at Calais with their telescopes. Then Ramsgate had been attacked too. Next came the Battle of Britain, with pitched battles being fought in the sky all over Kent. Biggin Hill, Gravesend and Deal had been bombed time and time again. One bomb even fell on the powerhouse of Betteshanger Colliery and its reluctant miners.

RAF Manston was nearly wiped off the map. Morale sank almost to zero. Civilians entered the ruined airfield and looted the damaged stores. A squadron leader had to grapple with another officer who was going to go into one of the air-raid shelters where the "erks" cowered and shoot the first airman who refused to come out, while the base chaplain had to reason with another officer who was going to shoot every one of his fellows lurking in the mess.

Biggin Hill was attacked by a force of low-flying Junkers, which swept in at 1,000 feet, bombing and machine-gunning. The first shelter was hit and no one survived; it was simply a smoking crater packed with dead airmen. The NAAFI and the WAAF quarters suffered an identical fate.

So it had gone on, week after week, month after month, year after year—twenty-one British fighters shot down in three short hours between Gravesend and the coast; four German spies landed between Hythe and Dungeness; parachute mines drifting down on Rochester, killing and injuring nearly a hundred citizens; Folkestone harbour badly damaged, again by mines, and a lance-corporal from Hull winning the BEM for diving into the harbour and rescuing a shot-down German pilot. For two years Kent had been in the front-line, its people praised by such dignitaries as Sir Auckland Geddes, Regional Commissioner in the South-East, for their "wonderful standard of resistance and discipline".

All that spring of 1942 the attacks had continued unrelentingly. They were mostly tip-and-run raids, but they caused death and misery all the same. Dover, which was in ruins, thousands sleeping nightly in its caves, was bombed yet again. Deal followed. The miners of Betteshanger Colliery had to spend eleven hours below ground because a bomb had destroyed the winding apparatus. A few days later it was Folkestone's turn once more. There seemed no end to the attacks on "the front line county", as the hard-pressed Kentish folk now called it. Yet in the midst of all this savagery and German fury, there was one city in Kent which had hitherto been untouched. That city was Canterbury.

To this day, nobody knows why the Germans had not attacked Canterbury before, when virtually every other major centre of population in Kent had been attacked in the previous two years. Many Germans were familiar with the city's role in the cultural history of England and the Continent. Chaucer's *Canterbury Tales* had long been translated into German and was used as a text in all the Reich's university English departments. The Germans also knew the work of Christopher Marlowe, one of the city's most celebrated sons, whose *Doctor Faustus* had been among the inspirations for Goethe's sublime play *Faust*. Moreover, the role of Canterbury as the premier see in England was also well known in Germany. The city might have no value as a military target— but that hadn't stopped the Luftwaffe from attacking places like Exeter.

But whatever the reasons that had prevented them from bombing Canterbury, the Germans now cast them aside. Cologne had swung the balance and the Führer wanted revenge.

Mrs Catherine Williamson, Lady Mayor of Canterbury since 1938, was fearful that the Sunday raid on Cologne would bring Hitler's wrath down upon her city. That evening she became increasingly anxious:

> I retired to my room, although I did not go to bed. Sitting on the edge of the bed, reading a book, I tried to while away the hours. All the other Baedeker raids had occurred at about 12.45am.[4]

She was not the only prominent citizen who was worried about what might be in store for the city that night. Dr William Temple, the Archbishop of Canterbury, was equally concerned. He had only recently been in York, missing the Baedeker raid there by days, and he reasoned that Canterbury was the next most obvious target for the Germans. He could only hope and pray that Canterbury would not suffer the same fate that had overtaken it back in 1011, when

126

a ruthless enemy had attempted to burn it down. But the Archbishop's prayers did not bear fruit. Before the night was over, one third of Canterbury's ancient centre had disappeared in fire and rubble.

Another anxious local was Kenneth Pinnock, a schoolmaster at Simon Langton Boys School. On fire duty at the school that Monday night, he found himself wondering what was to come after Cologne. For years now he'd been marking boys' essays entitled "My Most Memorable Experience", and "Nearly always I was rewarded by some story of how a bomber was shot down into the boy's back garden. . . . Their tales were lurid, unreliable and, as often as not, untrue."[5] But the dreams of those grubby boys of his English set were going to be realized at last. This time the German bombers were really coming to Canterbury.

While Pinnock pondered on what the night had in store for him and his fellow wardens, Norman Bacon of the RAF Regiment had just arrived at the city's West Station and was walking home through deserted streets. He had twenty-four hours' leave between postings and wanted to make the most of those precious hours. Later he recalled, "I never saw a soul apart from one warden and one policeman. I feel I must be unique. To be the last person to have walked the entire length of Canterbury as it had stood for centuries."[6] Norman Bacon was right. No one else would ever see the old city like that again. When he arrived home it was to find his wife very agitated. She had just heard Lord Haw-Haw on Radio Hamburg, sneering that Canterbury was going to be the Luftwaffe's next target.

This time the renegade was not lying. At quarter to one precisely the sirens started to wail, preceded by "Tugboat Annie", as the siren at the local gasworks was called. Almost immediately one lone plane crossed the old city, trailing flares behind it. Pinnock saw it at once, and "the sixteen blood-red flares dripping slowly from the sky, banishing the moonlight and transforming the familiar school buildings into a fantastic pattern of burning crimson and jet-black shadows".[7]

He called to his fellow fire-watcher, Mr Redman, "It's the real thing this time!"

At that moment a plane swooped in low. It had the familiar black crosses on its wings. "Jerry!" Redman cried. "We raced into one of the surface shelters and as we did so a rain of fire bombs spattered over the playground."[8] It had started.

Mrs Williamson had seen the Germans' arrival, too. As soon as the siren sounded, she rushed to the window and watched the falling flares illuminate the city with their "uncanny blue and yellow light". About three minutes later, she said, "there was an ominous sound of bombs dropping on the north side of the city".[9]

Unfortunately for Canterbury, those first bombs created a tragic deficiency in the city's Civil Defence. George Marks, who was both town clerk and ARP controller, was just about to make a dash for his post when his house was struck. Suddenly everything was confusion, noise, smoke and dust, as the house fell apart, trapping him and his wife beneath the rubble. He was dead. The city was now without a central controlling figure for the battle to come.

So, for one hundred and fifty terrible minutes, Canterbury was pounded from the air. Thousands of incendiaries tumbled down, setting fire to the ancient half-timbered houses. Soon, half the city centre was ablaze. No 57 St George Street, the birthplace of Christopher Marlowe, was gutted, as was the nearby house in Burgate Street where the nineteenth-century author of *The Ingoldsby Legends* had lived, the Reverend R. H. Barham. Lower Chantry Lane also disappeared, and with it the reputed home of the real Uriah Heep—"my 'umble 'ome" as he called it—and in St Dunstan's Street another house featured in Dickens's *David Copperfield* suffered the same fate.

In King's School, the Green Court and the medieval bakeries were hit. A young schoolboy who was destined for great things in this year of 1942 had once spent a miserable term here; his name was Bernard Law Montgomery. Everywhere parts of Britain's heritage were being destroyed in front of the eyes of the helpless, overworked Civil Defence workers.

Long ago, an early bishop of Canterbury, St Alphage, had appealed to an aggressor, "For your manhood's sake, do not make war on infants!" But that had been a thousand years before, when the pagans had responded to the bishop's plea. The new pagans had no such scruples. They dropped their bombs on infants as well as on defenceless men and women, boasting afterwards that they could "already see the flames from a dying Canterbury even as they took off from our fields in France".[10]

Ambulance driver Miss G. Hann was trying to make her way through the burning chaos. The planes were still swooping round over the city and dropping incendiaries, and as she later wrote "the whole city seemed ablaze from end to end". But young Miss Hann, who was also a trained nurse, had been summoned to collect a seriously wounded patient in her ambulance. Bravely she pressed on

128

through the flames. Then, approaching St Martin's Hill, she began to have her doubts; the hill was steep, there was so much rubble in the road, and flames too . . . "But," she concluded briskly, "there was no time to be lost with a patient waiting, so, changing down into low, I nursed the engine until we were by, just a little scorched by the fire."[11]

But all her courage was in vain. By the time Miss Hann reached the scene, her patient had died.

He was not the only one. Coming in on yet another wave, the German bombers were bringing with them more death and destruction. By now Pinnock and his fellow warden, Mr Redman, had left the surface shelter for an underground one, but even there they felt the terrifying blast of high explosive. "Won't they ever run out of bombs?" muttered Redman plaintively.[12]

Not yet, they wouldn't. Watching from her window, Mrs Williamson saw more and more planes arriving over Canterbury; the noise of engines overhead was "almost deafening", she said, and "it seemed as if the whole city was being laid flat."[13]

The Cathedral looked as though it would suffer the same fate. The heaviest bomb dropped by the Germans up to now, a tremendous four-ton monster filled with high explosive, fell only twenty yards from the entrance to the Warrior's Chapel. There was an ear-splitting explosion and the whole structure seemed to rock. Stained glass flew everywhere, mixed with fist-sized, red-hot lumps of shrapnel.

One observer, a veteran of the First World War, later recorded:

> By God's mercy the cathedral still stood four square, though vast craters gaped in its green precincts, and the walls and windows bore grievous scars—a desecration as vile as when Becket fell beneath his murderers' swordblades. But the eastern half of the High Street was in a condition only comparable to that of Ypres during the last war. It presented an almost unbroken vista of desolation, and among the buildings battered into shapeless rubble heaps or irreparably damaged were many hallowed by antiquity.[14]

The Archbishop himself had sheltered helplessly with his wife under the great oaken staircase of his residence. Now he ventured out to do what he could. But his sight was too poor and his movements too slow for the portly Dr Temple to be of much use. So he contented himself with bringing cups of tea to his servants in the Old Palace.

Later Dr Temple held a service "for the renewed dedication of our City to the service of God and of thankfulness for the spirit of its people in the recent time of trouble". But even now, when the true awfulness of the conflict was brought home to him, when he saw on his own doorstep the death and destruction which had been the lot of many British people for so long, he still could not bring himself to speak out against the enemy.

Little did he know, but Dr Temple was considered by the Germans to be an implacable opponent of the Third Reich. Before his appointment to the See of Canterbury, Goebbels had written of him in his diary:

> I have received confidential information concerning the probable successor to the Archbishop of Canterbury.[15] He will be Bishop Temple, who is much more dangerous than the old Canterbury gentleman [the then Archbishop, Cosmo Lang]. Temple is close to the Labour Party, was formerly a moderate friend of Germany, and is now a real German hater. He stands 100 percent behind Churchill, is clever at dialectics and, because of that fact, extremely dangerous. That means we may expect a number of severe attacks from the English clergy.[16]

Not only that. After the raids, the Gestapo spies reported to their masters in Berlin that Canterbury was widely regarded by ordinary German citizens to be "the seat of the notorious anti-German British archbishop".[17] But Goebbels and his spies need not have worried about Temple. As his biographer wrote: "During the next week Temple had to spend several nights in London, much as it distressed him to be away from the danger and from his wife."[18]

The German bombers were going and some of those below could now see comedy even in the midst of all the horror about them. A woman who had just given birth to a child had been handed a tin bowl and a towel at the beginning of the raid; these were both to be worn on the head, she was told, as there weren't enough tin hats. As she later remarked, "You can imagine what an amusing sight it was to see us women sitting up in bed with bowls on our heads, drinking cups of tea."[19]

Another woman stumbling out of her shelter to a transformed world found her budgie hopping around like a crazy thing in its cage, which was still hanging in the shambles of her living room. "Oh, my God!" she gasped; the bird had apparently turned white with the shock. Later, however, when she had recovered a little and had more time to examine the demented bird, she found it wasn't the shock of the raid which had turned the budgie white, but merely a bag of flour which had been thrown from the kitchen and had exploded in the living room!

Schoolmaster Kenneth Pinnock, emerging from the ruins of Simon Langton School, was more concerned with the survival of the school than anything else that morning.

> In the growing light we could see the playground. All over it were little white heaps where firebombs had burnt themselves out; there were great pieces of masonry and everywhere there was earth and stone. Not an inch of the original tarmac surface could be seen. I noted that some of the fire-bombs had stuck in the ground and stayed there without igniting.[20]

But Pinnock's spirits rose as the first rays of the sun touched the shattered ruins around him:

> Flame-coloured clouds parted to reveal Bell Harry Tower rising in queenly splendour over the awful scenes of ruin and desolation. It was a sight to revive one's shaken faith in the worth-whileness of human kind. Dawn had come; some of the city at any rate was still standing; *we were alive!*[21]

A similar mood of exultation was expressed by one of the boys at the school. At first the morning seemed to bode ill for young Porter, who felt "no dawn ever possessed such an ominous red tinge" as he waited for a bus to take him to school. But none came. A rumour started to circulate at the bus stop that all the buses had been burnt. Finally, however, a car stopped and gave Porter and another schoolboy a lift. Approaching Canterbury they grew tense. "It was like waiting for an examination result," Porter commented later. What awful sights would greet them in the city?

> And then we reached the top of St Thomas's Hill. I was aware of peering through the front window of the car—and seeing three towers . . . three towers standing triumphant amidst a sea of smoking ruins. An electric thrill ran through me, as when I hear the Hallelujah Chorus! It was the spirit of the medieval builder prevailing over the primeval destroyer. It was the symbol as to who should come victorious out of that Armageddon![22]

Fine, bold, defiant words from a teenage schoolboy, who is now a man nearing sixty. It was the kind of tone echoed by *The Times* that Monday, which, under the headline "REPRISAL RAID ON

CANTERBURY—CHURCHES AND SCHOOL DESTROYED", wrote: "The Fire Service and Civil Defence, helped by neighbouring districts, worked magnificently and the fires were soon under control.... Two churches, a newspaper office and two schools were among the buildings destroyed." Naturally, being *The Times*, they also had to mention the fact that "The Archbishop of Canterbury and Mrs Temple, who were in Canterbury during the raid, are safe. The Archbishop visited people in the town yesterday and inspected the damage."[23]

The bombing of Canterbury was speedily used by the Ministry of Information as a means of propaganda in neutral countries, particularly in America. The Duke of Kent, soon to be killed on active service, was instructed to tour the devastated city centre. He was the first of a stream of distinguished visitors, including Mrs Churchill and Mrs Roosevelt; the American President himself sent the usual gracious message, ending with "I wish to convey my deepest sympathy to those who were injured or suffered".[24]

Fortunately, they were not too many. Forty-three people were killed and another ninety-nine injured. But the damage to the historic city centre was dire and the heart of Canterbury, devoid of new buildings, was to lie waste for many years to come.

If London was pleased with the propaganda effect achieved by the attack on Canterbury—it was the first Baedeker city to be named immediately after a raid, on account of the fact that the city was known throughout the world—Berlin definitely was not. On 4 June, the same day the Duke of Kent made his visit to the stricken city, German police spies reported to their masters:

> The revenge attack on Canterbury at first occasioned general satisfaction among the population. However, when it was announced that the place had only 24,000 citizens and was without any military or economic importance, many voices were raised in disappointment.[25]

Furthermore, said the spies, the German people felt that Britain was getting the upper hand.

> The British seem to be going about the bombing of German cities in a systematic manner.... They [the German people] are asking why can't we retaliate in kind? Why can't we attack large British cities, for example, London, Bristol, Plymouth or Manchester? As long as this is not done, they think, the RAF terror attacks on German cities will continue.[26]

But there was little Hitler could do as the Baedeker spring of 1942 gave way to summer. His main concern was the new offensive in Central Russia, for which he needed every soldier, tank and aeroplane that he could scrape together. Little could be spared for large-scale air attacks on "perfidious Albion". As the head of the *Jagdwaffe*, the German Fighter Command, fighter pilot Adolf Galland wrote after the war:

> The material effect of this raid [on Canterbury] bore no comparison to the British raids. It was totally erroneous to expect such a strong effect on public morale that the English Command would be moved to stop their bomber offensive. In mitigation, however, one can perhaps take into account that, like the German people, Hitler, who initiated these retaliation raids, was also kept in ignorance of the actual strength of the attacker. Moreover, our own strength may have been given to him in exaggerated figures.[27]

So an impotent Hitler had to content himself with ordering a new heavy bomber to be put into production, which perhaps one day might carry the war back to England in the way Goering's Luftwaffe had done back in the great days of 1940. Meanwhile, his antiquated bombers continued to carry out minor attacks on other Baedeker cities.

Ipswich was raided, then Yarmouth, where St Nicholas's Parish Church, the largest in the country, was gutted; to Yarmouth St Nicholas's was what the Cathedral was to Norwich. But then pieces of Britain's cultural heritage were disappearing all the time now.

Norwich itself was raided yet again. Once more the locals feared for their Cathedral, but this time it was the Norfolk and Norwich Hospital that was hit. Margaret Lindley, then a student nurse, remembers helping to evacuate the 500 or so patients as smoke started to fill the wards:

> All my poor old men had left their false teeth on their lockers. We were not supposed to go back into the hospital, but my patients persuaded me and I crept back into the smoke-filled ward and collected several mugs of teeth—they had to sort out which belonged to who![28]

Bury St Edmunds had its raid, and a sugar factory was set on fire. Then it was Cambridge's turn, the raiders dropping incendiaries over Leys Road, Orchard Avenue and Arbury Road. A timber yard was set ablaze, with 114 houses being damaged. It wasn't much of a

"Baedeker" but now at last this cloistered home of academe could bear the proud scars of war.

But the Baedeker raids were about over. During the summer of 1942 enemy efforts dwindled to little more than nuisance raids on smaller towns and fringe targets. By August, the first round of this new kind of warfare was finished; and, although the Germans had surprised the British all along the line—cunningly selecting undefended targets, outwitting the defences technically, avoiding the RAF nightfighters sent up to intercept them—the British had won in the end.

Their victory, however, was due not so much to their own efforts, as to the fact that the enemy had not possessed the strength and resources to press home his advantage. As General Pile stated afterwards: "We couldn't win the first battle because we were never ready, so we made a virtue out of necessity and drew what comfort we could from the cliché."[29]

But all the same, a precedent had been created. Harris had started the ball rolling by selecting "soft targets" for his crews such as Lübeck and Rostock. The aim there had been as much to shake civilian morale as to damage targets of military importance. Cologne had followed as a demonstration of just how destructive an operation a thousand bombers could launch.

The Germans had retaliated in kind. They had made no effort to disguise the fact that the raids on York, Norwich or Canterbury were *Vergeltungsangriffe*—retaliation raids pure and simple. They had even stated so publicly, something that Harris would never have dared do, even at his most outspoken.

Now, for the time being at least, the Germans could do little to strike back at Britain. Secretly German scientists were working feverishly to perfect the most devastating reprisal weapons of all, the V-1 and V-2. But it would be another two years before these weapons made their appearance.

So for a while the field was left wide open for Harris and his men of Bomber Command. There remained sporadic criticism of what had become virtually unrestricted aerial warfare, but opponents of the policy were few: people like Richard Stokes, a Labour MP whose background was hardly pacifist (he had fought in the First World War and won the MC), or Bishop Bell, who in the coming year tried to make Temple call on the government for a statement on RAF bombing policy. Typically, however, Temple refused "to be the mouthpiece of the concern which I know exists, because I do not share it".[30]

There were even individual protests in the Reich, as Douglas Bartlett, manager of W. H. Smith's in Canterbury, discovered just after the war. Visiting the Rhineland, he met an ex-Luftwaffe pilot who had taken part in the raid on Canterbury; and after the raid, the pilot told him, his wife had declared a "*Sex-Streik*" in protest, refusing to sleep with him thereafter![31]

But they were the exceptions. The bomber commanders knew no such scruples. Besides, their cause was being furthered by the "Johnnies-come-lately" who were beginning to arrive by the thousand. The previous year their military attaché had declared proudly, "I cannot see how the British Empire can defeat Germany without the help of God or Uncle Sam. Perhaps it will take both!"[32] In what was to come, God would play not the slightest role.

SIX

On Saturday, 26 January, 1942, Private First Class Milburn H. Henke stepped ashore at Dufferin Quay, Belfast, to find himself faced by a dazzling array of British dignitaries: the Duke of Abercorn; the Prime Minister of Northern Ireland; Sir Archibald Sinclair, the Minister of Air, in his old-fashioned wing collar; and the three service chiefs in Ulster, all there to welcome *him*! For Henke was the first American soldier to land on British soil since the end of the First World War.

Sir Archibald launched into a speech about the thousands of American soldiers now heading for Britain "not to sojourn among strangers but among grateful friends. Their safe arrival marks a new stage in the war . . ."[1] The speeches went on and on, as Henke shifted from one foot to the other, until finally the strains of a military band and the soft-shoe shuffle of many Americans marching could be heard from a nearby road. All heads craned round and faces flushed with embarrassment. Despite the welcoming committee's plans, a large contingent of American GIs had already landed and were marching off to their new camp. Instead of being the first American soldier of the Second World War to land in Britain, poor Henke was the 501st! To add insult to injury, he was later interviewed by a radio reporter whom Henke took to be from the American NBC but who was in fact from the BBC. Asked how he felt, Henke obliged with what he thought an American listening audience would like to hear and blurted out, "*Gee, Mom, I sure wish I was back home again!*"[2]

The Yanks, as the British invariably called them, regardless of which side of the Mason-Dixon Line they came from, had arrived and for the average Briton they were an eye-opener. They were brash and bold. They put an un-English zest into everything. They were no respecters of persons or traditions. To the British quip that they were "over-paid, over-fed, over-sexed—and *over here!*" they would snap back, "Yeah, because you are under-paid, under-fed, under-sexed—and under Eisenhower!"

With them the Americans brought a host of innovations: Coca-Cola, baseball (a game for girls, as far as the British were concerned), candy bars, nylons and chewing gum. "Got any gum, chum?" soon became the catch-phrase among small British boys. They also brought with them an overweening confidence in themselves, which seemed to find its expression in their relentless, and successful, pursuit of the local women. "We've got thirty thousand rubbers in the supply room," one former GI recalls his supply sergeant announcing one morning after reveille. "I want you people to do something about this!"[3] The gleeful company of GIs, who were being offered something like three hundred contraceptives per man, were only too happy to oblige!

Even their top brass was different. Lieutenant-General Carl "Tooey" Spatz, who commanded the Eighth Air Force, had a face like a rusty nail and scorned uniforms. Patton once took him to task for not having shaved, while Eisenhower ordered him to make his airmen salute properly. Spatz retorted that saluting didn't matter as long as his men did their job correctly.

Although Spatz did not get on well with most of the RAF's top brass, whom he thought "stuffy", he did see eye to eye with his opposite number in Bomber Command. Like Harris, Spatz took it as an article of faith that heavy bombers, correctly used, could bring about the defeat of Nazi Germany and make the invasion of the Continent unnecessary. Both men thought that the aeroplane was the war-winning weapon.

They did, however, differ as to how the heavy bomber should be employed. The Americans had studied the German blitz on Britain seriously and concluded that it might well have succeeded if it had been better planned. In 1942, however, America's leading expert on air power, Russian-born Major Alexander Seversky, made the following point:

> Another vital lesson—one that has taken even air specialists by surprise—relates to the behaviour of civilian populations under air punishment. It had been generally assumed that serial bombardment would quickly shatter popular morale, causing

deep civilian reactions. . . . The progress of this war has tended to indicate that this expectation was unfounded. . . .

These facts are significant beyond their psychological interest. They mean that haphazard destruction of cities— sheer blows at morale—are costly and wasteful in relation to the tactical results achieved. . . . Unplanned vandalism from the air must give way, more and more, to planned, predetermined destruction. More than ever the principal objectives will be the critical aggregrates of electric power, aviation industries, dock facilities, essential public utilities and the like.[4]

This was where Spatz, a follower of Seversky, differed radically from Harris. He and his fellow USAAF generals felt that, although civilian casualties were acceptable in the course of "precision bombing", as the new strategy was called, the deliberate mass slaughter of civilians was not.

Thus, as the US Eighth Air Force flew its first mission—a "milk run" attack on the marshalling yards at Rouen on 17 August, 1942—two different bombing strategies were beginning to emerge, with the Americans confident that theirs was the right one. As General Ira Eaker, Spatz's subordinate, said, the USAAF policy of "completely dislocating German industry and commerce" would allow them to "remove from the enemy the means of waging successful warfare".[5] A bold prediction. It took a year for that bubble of American optimism to be burst.

Two weeks after the Americans' attack on Rouen the 1,000-bomber strike force which had brought Harris his first great victory was quietly dismantled. For the rest of the year Bomber Command settled down to a steady pounding of Germany on a broad front. The new campaign was less spectacular and brought less dramatic results than the massive raid on Cologne, but it was costly and it hardened the young airmen who conducted it. This was the second generation of aircrews; most of their predecessors had already been killed or, if lucky, promoted. By early 1943 the RAF had suffered 40,000 fatalities—more than the whole of the British Army at that date.

The aircrews settled down to the new routine and soon grew used to the strangely inverted timetable. In their temporary camps in Yorkshire and Lincolnshire (the Canadians and in some cases the Americans were taking over the permanent, pre-war RAF stations), the young men woke late. Mess hours had been relaxed for the

NCOs and officers on flying duty and they would straggle over for breakfast long after the "desk-wallahs" were at work. Thereafter they'd hang about, playing darts or reading the papers, waiting to hear whether an "op" was on for the coming night. If not, they would rush away to the local fleshpots, such as they were.

If an "op" was on, however, then they would watch from the windows of their Nissen huts as the ground crew "erks" went about their business, fuelling and arming the planes. There would be a brief air test of the planes; then, at nightfall, they attended the briefing session. They collected their mascots and clambered aboard, staggering under the weight of their kit.

Night after night it went on until they had completed their tour of "ops"—or until fate overtook them. Then the regimental policemen, under the direction of the station adjutant, would spirit their bits and pieces out of their lockers before too many of the other crews knew what had happened; in a few minutes all trace of them would have vanished as if they had never existed.

From time to time, some of them cracked. The Rev Harry Radcliffe, who had survived the York Baedeker raid to become an RAF chaplain, was once asked by a station commander to talk to a young pilot who had "gone yellow", refusing to fly on his first operation. Radcliffe managed to talk the shaken young man into going: "But he never came back from that raid. It is something that I shall remember to my dying day."[6]

Some couldn't be talked or even threatened into going. Exactly how many men refused to fly or broke under the strain is still a closely guarded secret. The Ministry of Defence will say nothing on the matter and there appear to be no relevant documents in the Public Record Office. A few individuals made their standpoint quite clear; they were scared and that was that. They were court-martialled, stripped of their rank and speedily transferred to the infantry. Others were sent to what were little better than detention centres, like the one at Sheffield, where strict discipline and a period of square-bashing would, it was believed, make them willing to fly operationally again.

But they all undoubtedly suffered to some extent under the constant strain, a strain compounded by the fact that they couldn't admit to feeling "windy"—for in 1942 it was still considered unmanly to confess that you were scared.

Shortly before the 1,000-bomber raid on Cologne a secret report prepared by the medical officer on one operational station, who had studied aircrew for two years, stated that there were three distinct stages in the men's attitude to flying. The first was when they were "raring to go". In the second stage they would be "willing but not volunteering". In the last stage, just before they completed a tour of duty, they would be definitely unwilling—but would not say so. The unknown officer concluded: "Aircrew are placed in a psychologically impossible position and every pilot without exception will, in the end, develop an anxiety neurosis. It is inexorable and inevitable."[7]

"The only wounds the Yanks ever get are from frostbite!" the RAF mocked the US Eighth Air Force. In their heavily-armoured "ships", which carried one third of the bomb load of the average British bomber, they flew at a tremendously high altitude. Indeed, the Americans' early raids were so insignificant that the total of bombs dropped was announced in the official communiqués in pounds rather than tons. Their losses were also very low. From their first sortie in August, 1942, to the end of the year, the Eighth Air Force mounted twenty-seven raids on Europe, losing only thirty-two aircraft, less than two per cent.

A British boffin who flew with them thought the American aircrew "all very raw and young and . . . rather cocky. They had come to make mincemeat of the Huns. . . . They didn't want advice. Their Fortresses were invincible."[8]

Despite their claims for the Norden bombsight, which had worked excellently in the cloudless skies of the Southern United States but which was useless in an European autumn, the Americans had scattered their bombs in an alarming manner among the French civilians living around their targets. Indeed, half their sorties were uncompleted. Moreover, they had not yet met the "first team", as they called the Germans. They still had not crossed the borders of the Reich. The horrors of Flak Valley (the Ruhr) were as yet unknown to them.

All the same, in spite of the poor results achieved by the Americans, the British fell over themselves to be complimentary. The Secretary of State for Air, Sir Archibald Sinclair, eulogized "the prodigies of daylight bombing which the US Bomber Air Force have already begun to achieve".[9] Harris made repeated warm references to them, unusual in a man of his prickly nature, and constantly supported Spatz in his demands for more aircraft and crews.

Thus the Americans spent their first winter overseas learning to drink lukewarm beer and play darts in the local pub, generous to a fault with their money and the "goodies" with which they were so liberally supplied. For the people of the rural areas of Norfolk and East Anglia, where they were mainly stationed, they were an eye-opener. The locals noted, too, that they were quite unlike the RAF aircrews who had flown from some of the stations earlier in the war. They were homesick and admitted it. They were afraid, and they admitted that too!

Commenting on the Americans' lack of inhibition, one eighteen-year-old Red Cross worker later said:

> There was no stiff upper lip. If it had been a good raid with few lost there was a happy atmosphere, but if it was a bad one, a terrible air of depression hung over the whole place. It was always so quiet, no piano, no whistling, no radio, they talked quietly together, if at all. . . . Sometimes they would talk to us about it, about the flak, or the altitude they flew at—they suffered badly from sinus if they were too high for too long. . . . They were really upset about losing aircraft, some would even break down and cry. . . . We had to get them away into the sick bay quickly. An upset like that could spread so very quickly.[10]

Another woman remembered a young American air gunner named Pickles who had been brought to her house in a bad way. She gave him a cup of tea and "found he couldn't hold the cup steady":

> His hand was shaking, his eyes blinked every few seconds. . . . He was a rear gunner in one of those big planes and . . . before the night was out he was crying with his head in my lap. I stroked his head and felt like his mother. He cried for his mom and I cried with him. I gently laid him on the couch, covered him with a blanket and sang to him. He slept and I went to bed. Next morning I got up and Pickles was gone. I never saw him again. He was killed on his next mission.[11]

But as time passed the Americans grew harder and tougher. Now they were flying across the borders of the Reich to attack German cities and their losses were beginning to mount. On 27 January, 1943, attacking their first German target, Wilhelmshaven, the Eighth lost three out of fifty-three bombers. Two months later, striking nearby Bremen, they lost sixteen out of a hundred B-17s. Morale started to drop. It sank even lower when, due to the shortage of replacements, General Spatz was forced to raise the number of missions per tour from twenty-five to thirty. Whole squadrons were being wiped out—especially if the squadron happened to occupy "Purple Heart Corner", the bottom rear corner of the Flying Fortresses' box-like flight formation. This was the favourite target of the German fighters and the most likely spot for an airman to win a Purple Heart.

All the same, the American losses could in no way match those of Bomber Command, which had been battering away at the most heavily defended part in the whole of the Reich—the Ruhr Valley. Throughout that winter of 1942–43 Harris's men had attacked the industrial towns of the Ruhr time and time again.

They had flown a record 18,506 sorties, losing 872 aircraft. This was a loss of nearly five per cent, with a further sixteen per cent damaged. That was the average. Some nights thirty per cent of the planes failed to return.

Such losses were deeply worrying for Harris, particularly as the raids had not achieved the spectacular results he had predicted. Besides, Bomber Command was losing its public appeal, as new stars came along, like Montgomery and his Eighth Army, which had just won Britain's first real victory on land at El Alamein. Bomber Command needed another great success like the raid on Cologne, which would make it headline news again. It was then, as Harris reviewed his tactics and pondered on the growing strength of the German defenders, that his air staff pressed him to consider using a new and highly secret technical device code-named "Window".

Window was simply a bundle of metal strips which could be pushed out of an aircraft, usually the one leading the bomber stream, at the rate of one bundle per minute. This created a kind of smokescreen effect which baffled enemy radar operators on the ground and in the air.

It was a technical break-through, but one which Professor Lindemann, or Lord Cherwell as he had just become, had hitherto succeeded in banning the RAF from using. He argued that the Germans might well use a similar device, after they had discovered what it was, against Britain's own defences. But now, the Baedeker raids having degenerated into small-scale attacks on fringe targets, Harris began to urge the use of the new device.

But Lord Cherwell remained doubtful and it took months to convince him. In the end he agreed but then Fighter Command objected. They didn't want Window to be used until Sicily had been invaded in July, 1943. Herbert Morrison, the Home Secretary, was also opposed to its use. He was always nervous of the effect of German raids on the civilian population. He knew that the political future of many of his cronies in the local London councils hung in the balance, because their boroughs held them responsible for the inadequate provisions they had made for the blitzes on the capital.

Eventually, on 23 June, 1943, just as Harris's Ruhr campaign was coming to an end, a final conference was held under Churchill himself to decide whether or not Window should be used.

Among the advocates of Window that day was Dr R. V. Jones. Just before the conference started, he noticed an "individual in a boiler suit" come padding into the room. Jones took him for "a Ministry of Works maintenance engineer who had inadvertently strayed into a room full of Generals while looking for some domestic installation" and thought "it seemed kindest to pretend not to notice the chap". But then, to Jones's surprise, the "maintenance engineer" turned to the young scientist and growled in that unmistakable voice, "Very glad to have you here, Jones."[12] It was Churchill, dressed in his famous siren suit.

The brass got down to business. Jones stated his case for Bomber Command. Churchill listened carefully, then turned to Leigh Mallory, the head of Fighter Command, and asked him what he thought. Mallory said that, if the device was used against the United Kingdom and the defences failed, it was Fighter Command that would have to "carry the can"; nevertheless, he recognized that the priority now was to reduce Bomber Command's casualties. He agreed that Window should be used.

That concluded the argument and Churchill declared, in characteristic style, "Very well, let us open the Window!"[13]

Morrison made one last try to have the use of the device stopped, threatening to raise the matter in the War Cabinet. But Churchill overruled him. He growled that the device was too technical for the War Cabinet to understand and announced that he personally would take responsibility for the decision to use Window. It was to be used from 23 July onwards.

SEVEN

INTENTION: To destroy Hamburg. *INFORMATION*: The total destruction of this city would achieve immeasurable results in reducing the industrial capacity of the enemy's war machine. This, together with the effect on German morale, which would be felt throughout the country, would play a very important part in shortening and in winning the war. The Battle of Hamburg cannot be won in a single night. It is estimated that at least 10,000 tons of bombs will have to be dropped to complete the process of elimination. . . . Bomber Command forces will consist of all available heavies in operational squadrons until sufficient hours of darkness enable the medium bombers to take part.[1]

This order for mass destruction, Command Operation Order No 173, had been on file at every RAF Bomber Group headquarters since 27 May, 1943. But the ban on using Window had stopped Harris from carrying out the plan to wipe out Germany's second largest city. He knew that Hamburg was so well defended that, without Window, his bomber force would be decimated. Besides, the Combined Chiefs of Staff had decided, one month before Command Operation Order No 173 had been sent to the Groups, that "the first priority in the operation of British and American bombers based in the United Kingdom shall be accorded to the attack on German fighter forces and the industry upon which they depend".[2]

For the US Eighth Air Force was now taking so many casualties over Germany, due to the bold attacks of German fighter squadrons, that it had been decided that only cities producing fighter planes or their component parts should be bombed. Hamburg, however, produced ships (including forty-five per cent of Germany's submarines); out of its 3,000 factories and 5,000 commercial enterprises, only two manufactured aeroplane components. Germany's second city was therefore precluded as a possible target.

But Harris, to whom the original draft of the Combined Chiefs' order had been sent, had managed to insert a final sentence into the original which read:

> While the forces of the British Bomber Command will be employed in accordance with their main aim in the general disorganization of German industry, their action will be designed as far as practicable to be complementary to the operations of the Eighth Air Force.[3]

This sentence, which the Combined Chiefs accepted, marked an important concession. Harris would otherwise have been committed to supporting the Americans' unsound strategy of *exclusively* bombing aircraft targets. As Harris reasoned, virtually every large German city contained some product potentially useful to the Luftwaffe. So those two lonely factories manufacturing parts for the German Air Force justified him in ordering the attack on Hamburg—"Operation Gomorrah" as it was code-named.

And now Harris had Window. On 15 July, 1943, he finally received the permission he had been waiting for all winter. Two days later he issued his order to attack Hamburg. Churchill had authorized the device to be used from 23 July. Harris ordered his bombers to attack on the night of the 22nd/23rd, with the first bundle of Window to be dropped at exactly *one minute after midnight!*

In the event, however, he was unable to cock a snook at the Establishment, for the weather that night was unsuitable. But Saturday, 24 July dawned fine and sunny, both in eastern England and north-west Germany, and the meteorologists predicted that weather conditions would be ideal. In northern Germany they had had a splendid July, dry and warm, so the older houses in Hamburg, most with wooden beams, would be as dry as tinder. With a bit of luck, the bombers could start a blaze to rival the great fire of 1842, which had nearly burned Hamburg to the ground. That morning Harris gave out his orders. Operation Gomorrah was on.

For weeks now the RAF had been dropping leaflets over Hamburg, warning people to abandon the city while there was still time. But Claus Fuhrmann, who had been dismissed from his job because his mother was Jewish and was now living a hand-to-mouth existence in the port, was not over-concerned. Like his fellow citizens, he had heard it all before. "Everyone was too used to official exaggeration to take anything seriously."[4] So no one paid much attention to the RAF's warning.

Another person who believed that nothing would happen to her was 63-year-old Frau Mathilde Wolff-Moenckeberg. She belonged to a prominent local family (one of Hamburg's most famous streets, the Moenckebergstrasse, is named after the family) and had a daughter who was married to a British university lecturer, living in Wales. Later, in a letter to her daughter she wrote:

> For weeks beforehand we had reconnaissance planes over night after night, but without shooting. We always dressed very quickly, but then sat in the library, suitcases packed and ready by the front door. We were told the British would avoid Hamburg because they would need the town and its harbour later on and we lived in a fool's paradise. We listened with horror to reports about the frightful raids on Cologne, Essen, Bochum, etc. . . . Descriptions were so ghastly that one could hardly believe them. Yet we still thought we would be safe, even when the leaflets were dropped: *"You have got a few weeks' respite, then it will be your turn. There is peace now, then it will be eternal peace!"*[5]

Berlin housewife Else Wendel, who had just arrived in Hamburg, was less complacent. She had been through the raids on Berlin and had experienced their full horror. Once she had seen a block of flats in Berlin which had been struck by a stick of English bombs:

> What happened in the flats was too terrible to be printed. The tenants had not been burned but scalded to death. The water pipes of the central heating system had burst and boiling water had poured into the air-raid shelter. They found women with their arms stretched out holding their children above their heads as they died. They found people crouched on the tops of piles of chairs and tables as they clambered to escape the rising boiling water. No wonder they didn't print these facts at the time.[6]

But Else Wendel was the exception. Hamburg's citizens had lived through 134 bombing raids, which had had little effect on the life of the city, and the last air raid had been over a year before. Since then, the sirens had occasionally sounded as RAF reconnaissance planes flew over the city; but, as one commentator later wrote,

> The citizens took this in their stride. They made their way in a routine manner to the shelters and the few overhead bunkers, such as the one in St Pauli, in the city's red-light district, taking with them their cases containing the essentials. Even small children carried bags to the shelters where they continued their sleep on a blanket. People cursed the nightly disturbance and wished the night-fighters would shoot down a few "Tommies" and put an end to the "nuisance". Little did they guess what was soon coming their way.[7]

Holme-on-Spalding Moor, home of the RAF's 76th Squadron, just south of the little town of Market Weighton, was a dreary kind of station set in rural East Yorkshire. The "natives" were surly farm labourers, for the most part, who didn't take too kindly to the fast-living young officers and NCOs who had been dumped down in their midst back in 1940. By the summer of 1942 some of the surliness seemed to have rubbed off on the men of the 76th, for, despite their high jinks in the mess, they appeared an unhappy, truculent Squadron; and they had good cause to be. They had lost a steady one or two aircraft per raid for months and their morale was shaky. Every week new faces appeared—and disappeared just as rapidly.

As one of the pilots said after the war:

> The atmosphere in the Flight Office would be very tense until the news came through. Completely contrary to the popular impression given in books and films, there would be a relieved cheer, loud laughter and a babble of excited talk if we were not to operate that day. If we were due to do so, the pilots would merely make some casual remark and quickly slip away to get themselves, their aircraft and crews ready. Later we would return to learn what the target would be—not without some secret dread in our hearts that it might again be Berlin or the Ruhr.[8]

But on the Saturday evening of 24 July, as the veterans and new boys of 76th Squadron were briefed on their target for the night, they learned it wasn't going to be Berlin or the Ruhr. Instead, 791 aircraft were going to attack the port of Hamburg. That news didn't bring much relief, however, for the veterans knew Hamburg was well defended by flak and night-fighters, and the flight was almost as long as the one to Berlin.

The next bit of information brought a ray of hope. A startling new top-secret device was going to be used on the raid for the first time. It was called Window. It was nothing more than bundles of metal foil strips, which the wireless operator and flight operator were going to throw out of the aircraft through a special chute at intervals during their run over Germany. But these strips of foil, they were assured by the "staff wallah" from 4 Group Operational Research, based at Heslington Hall, York, would fog up every Hun radar screen—guns, night-fighters, the lot. The German defenders would be fighting the attackers totally blind.

All over north-eastern England and East Anglia, other staff officers were reading out the same statement to bemused aircrews:

> Tonight you are going to use a new and simple counter-measure, Window, to protect yourselves against the German defence system. . . . The German defences will, therefore, become confused and you should stand a good chance of getting through unscathed.[9]

Outside the ground crews were already loading each aircraft with huge numbers of small parcels, which they had been strictly ordered not to open. Not that they were concerned. They assumed the parcels contained the usual leaflets.

At exactly quarter to twelve that Saturday night the first two-engined Stirling took off from an airfield in Cambridgeshire. For the next hour and a quarter, laden with 1,454 tons of high explosive and 1,006 tons of incendiaries—a staggering 350,000 fire bombs in all—the rest of the great bomber force was taking off from forty-two different fields.

In three streams they crossed the English coast at Hornsea, Mablethorpe and Cromer. Eighty miles off the German coast, at the predetermined "Position A", they began to form up. For the last leg of the flight they would fly on the same course and at the same speed, though at different heights, guided to their target by various technical devices, in particular the H2S radar aid. Navigators in the leading planes peered into the apparatus, waiting for the first appearance of the shimmering green shape of the coastline on the cathode tube. There it was! Then they watched for the black snake-like ribbon of the River Elbe, which would lead them straight to their target. As Dudley Saward described that moment,

> The River Elbe was deliberately unfolding itself as far as Hamburg, displaying, with vagueness at first, but later with detailed clarity, the bright fringes of the dock area. As the city of Hamburg approached the centre of the tube it became more and more doomed.[10]

They had been dropping Window ever since they left Position A, each bomber following the lead of the first Pathfinder aircraft. One officer later described how he watched "these little strips streaming past me and disappearing into the darkness"; it was, he said, like "a shoal of river fish darting along in murky water".[11]

The results were better even than the British boffins had anticipated. Searchlights were wandering drunkenly all over the sky as the Germans searched for the raiders in vain. The flak gunners wrung their hands helplessly. The night-fighters could not come within miles of the great stream of bombers. Despite the clear night, the defenders were sightless, like blind men groping clumsily for an opponent.

Back at the listening station at Kingsdown, Kent, Dr R. V. Jones was delighted.

> We heard one German controller get fixed on this stuff which obviously was not an aircraft and telling it to waggle its wings and so forth, without any success. When another controller saw extra aircraft appearing where only one had been before, he burst into indignation over the radio, "*The English bombers are propagating themselves!*" and then we heard a quite different voice taking command and I wondered whether it might be Goering himself and it turned out it was![12]

It was all great fun for the observers on the ground in Britain, but for General Kammhuber, commander of the German radar defence line named after him—*die Kammhuber-Linie*—it was an absolute nightmare. He soon learned that the seven night-fighter boxes allotted to the defence of Hamburg had been thrown into total confusion by Window. As he later admitted, "The whole defence was blinded at one stroke." Confused night-fighter pilots, relying wholly on their airborne radar for location of their target, found themselves apparently surrounded by British bombers, but without a single machine in sight.

And all the while the bombers flew on towards their unsuspecting target, guided on their way by the yellow marker flares dropped by Air Marshal Bennett's Pathfinder Force, heading straight for the aiming point: a feature located halfway between the River Elbe and Hamburg's city lake, the Binnenalster, where once its citizens had taken their summer pleasures on warm July nights such as this but which was now covered by a vast camouflage net. The object was to destroy a huge area of central Hamburg, three miles by one and a half, concentrating not only on the docks and factories which lined the banks of the Elbe, but also on the busy red-light district of St Pauli and the Reeperbahn and the residential area around the Hauptbahnhof, the main station. Harris intended this first raid of the "new era" to continue his old policy of "de-housing" the enemy. That euphemism concealed one of the most vicious attacks on civilians ever recorded.

At thirty-three minutes after midnight on that Saturday morning, 25 July, the sirens sounded Hamburg's 319th alarm. A policeman stationed on a water tower near the Elbe noted that everything "glowed in a bright white light", as the flares started to drop in profusion. But he, like the other million-odd citizens of Germany's second largest city, was not particularly alarmed. They had been through it all before. Why should this raid be any different from hundreds that had preceded it?

"I still remember every detail of the hot July night when the first large-scale raid began," Claus Fuhrmann recalled years later:

> At first there was nothing unusual about it; people sat cowering in their damp cellars, children wept, the whistle of falling bombs, dull thudding hits, blasts of air which tore out windows and doors. . . . But what was new was the way it went on; while red flames stood above the houses and the air was black with dust and dirt and the fire engines were clanging through the streets, the sirens went again. With a deep zooming sound, the squadrons returned to the city. Again the sharp clear bark of 88mm guns alternated with the deep, powerful hits of heavy bombs.
>
> At first I was not caught in the general mood of panic. "The British don't mean me," I thought. I had nothing to fear. Those men up there in the sky were fighting against the Nazis too; we had the same enemy. However stupid it may sound, I felt instinctively that no British bomb could harm me. I was firmly resolved to stay in Hamburg and see what happened. I wanted to witness the death of the city.[13]

Claus Fuhrmann, who had lost his job due to the Nazis and had found himself a fugitive in his own native city, survived to see just that; but many of his fellow citizens did not. Before the week was out, over 40,000 of the citizens of Hamburg were dead.

The bombers came in six waves, one following the other in perfect timing. The whole business was over within fifty-five minutes (five minutes longer than planned), bomber after bomber raining down his load of death and destruction on the virtually defenceless city.

"The light flickers and flickers, but doesn't go out yet," Frau Wolff-Moenckeberg wrote to her daughter in Wales:

> The house shakes, the windows tremble and it is completely different from any of the other times. . . . All you can see is fire. No one speaks. Tense faces wait for the worst of every gargantuan explosion. Heads go down automatically when-ever there is a crash and features are trapped in horror. . . . At last it gets quieter; the inferno recedes into the distance. Back in our flat we stand on the balcony and see nothing but a circle of flames around the Alster, fire everywhere in our neighbourhood. Thick clouds of smoke are hanging over the city and smoke comes in through all the windows carrying large flakes of fluttering ash. And it is raining in torrents! We go into the road just for a moment at 3.30 am. In the Sierichstrasse several houses have collapsed and fire is still raging. The sight of the Bellevue is dreadful and the Muhlenk-amp is nothing but glass and rubble. We go to bed completely shattered.[14]

The old lady was lucky. As the early sun tried to fight its way through the heavy smoke which lay over the city, the rescue workers and firemen still toiled desperately at their tasks. This one raid had killed and injured more people than all the Baedeker raids put together. Over 1,500 were dead and nearly 5,000 had been seriously injured. Thousands had been rendered homeless.

Everywhere flats and houses lay in ruins or were on fire. Properties ranging from the birthplace of Brahms to the famed Hagenbeck Zoo had been destroyed. Zoo-keepers were seen weeping as they carried out dead monkeys on stretchers, and the local inhabitants of Hamburg-Stelling, where the Zoo was located, marvelled at how the wild animals "waited patiently to be shut up again when their cages were blown open, except for the monkeys which swarmed, chattering excitedly over the ruins of the surround-ing streets".[15]

This incident later provided Goebbels with useful propaganda material. The long-established newspaper, *Hamburger Anzeiger*, which was under his control, asked in feigned bewilderment, "What made this place of research, education and entertainment, well known all over the world, an attractive target for the enemy?"[16]

In truth, Goebbels and the rest of the Nazi *Prominenz* had much more serious problems than the fate of Hagenbeck Zoo on their minds, as the full extent of the damage to Hamburg began to be revealed that Sunday. The city was suffering the very fate that Hitler had conceived for London back in 1940, when he had ranted that he wanted:

> fires everywhere. Thousands of them! Then they'll unite in one gigantic conflagration. Goering has the right idea. Explosive bombs don't work but it can be done with incendiary bombs—total destruction of London![17]

Well, London had not been destroyed. But the 300,000 incendiary bombs which had been dropped on Hamburg that Sunday morning were well on their way to destroying the city. Speer said that Hamburg had "put the fear of God into me!" At the end of the week he told the Central Planning Committee that if the air raids on Hamburg continued on the same scale, "within three months we shall be relieved of a number of questions we are at present discussing". In other words, Germany would have lost the war. And so, Speer concluded, "We might as well hold the final meeting of Central Planning, in that case."[18]

According to Goebbels, Hamburg's *Gauleiter* Kaufmann was in a panic.

> Kaufmann, in his first report, spoke of a catastrophe the extent of which simply staggers the imagination. A city of a million inhabitants has been destroyed in a manner unparalleled in history. We are faced with problems that are almost impossible of solution. I believe Kaufmann has lost his nerve somewhat in the face of this situation.[19]

Kaufmann was not the only one. Goebbels' police spies reported that day from Hanover, some 120 miles from Hamburg, that the Senior Burgomaster of Gottingen, who had just stepped out of a train from Hamburg in full uniform, was attacked by a mob, being accounted one of those responsible for what had happened in Hamburg.

A woman thrust a sleeve in front of his nose and said, couldn't he smell the stink of gas [from the bombs]? Perhaps he hadn't experienced a bombing raid yet? One day they would pay him and his kind back for what they had just suffered.[20]

Goering, who bore more responsibility than most for what had happened, flinched from confronting the awful reality. Once he had loved to display himself in front of the workers and ordinary people with whom he had been immensely popular. Now he made no attempt to visit the stricken city until long after the raids were over, and when he did go he soon regretted it. For everywhere he went, he was greeted by jeering mobs. He never went back to Hamburg again.

Nor did Hitler go, of course, although he was advised to by Speer. Hitler, unlike Churchill, never visited any of his bombed cities; not once during the course of the whole war did he show any sympathy with the suffering citizens of Germany.

But some of Goering's subordinate officers did draw their conclusions from this raid and those to come. A week after they were over and the balance sheet had been drawn up, Goering's closest associate and Chief-of-Staff for four years, General Jeschonnek, was found dead in his office. He had committed suicide. Later General Milch, Inspector-General of the Luftwaffe, told Speer that Jeschonnek had not wished Goering to attend his funeral; that had been explicit in the brief note he had left. (Goering did attend, though; there would have been a public scandal if he hadn't.)

Milch, too, was in despair. At a conference of senior Luftwaffe officers called to discuss the Hamburg raid, he declared in a broken voice, "We have lost the war. I tell you—we have lost the war."[21]

EIGHT

At 4.26 p.m. that Sunday afternoon the Americans also raided Hamburg. But they weren't as lucky as the British had been the night before. They ran into trouble the moment they crossed the coast. This time there was no Window to fool the enemy, and packs of Me-109s and Focke-Wulfs were waiting for the USAAF's 123 Flying Fortresses.

The crews of the 384th Bomber Group from Grafton-Underwood suffered the most as the German fighter pilots came swooping in, firing at them at point-blank range. Of the 544th Squadron, only one of the seven bombers in the formation survived the approach to Hamburg. One after another the planes succumbed to the attacks.

As the flank of the "box" became exposed, the German fighters relentlessly pressed home their attack. Time and again they came zooming in, cannon chattering, as gunners in the open bays swung their half-inch machine guns around to meet the challenge. Some were so badly damaged that they had to turn back. When one of them landed at Grafton-Underwood its crew were found lying on the floor in pools of blood, while another slewed across the runway and braked to a stop, engines still running. No one got out.

However, most of the American crews pressed home their attack, concentrating on finding their targets: the Blohm and Voss U-boat yard and the Kloeckner aero-engine plant. But the persistent enemy interference had had its effect. As the sirens once again sent Hamburg's citizens scrambling for the shelters, the Americans began to drop their bombs—but their aim was not true. Once again the unfortunate Hagenbeck Zoo suffered; three wagon-loads of animals were hit while waiting at the railway station to be transported to the safety of Vienna Zoo.

The Americans began heading out across the North Sea in the hope that the German fighters, with their limited range, would not pursue them over the water. One such fleeing plane was "Weary Willie", which had already been ripped to shreds by German cannon fire. The Fortress was in a pitiful state. Three engines were hit and smoking badly, the supply of oxygen had been shot away, the navigator and bombardier had both been wounded by a cannon shell that exploded inside the plane, and now the gunners' ammunition ran out. The plane was crippled and defenceless. But the pilot was determined to bring his "ship" home. Falling out of formation, he dodged six attacking Focke-Wulfs in a spectacular dive to 5,000 feet. The fuselage groaned as if it might fall apart at any moment. But the dodge worked and the enemy fighters disappeared.

In the end the pilot had to ditch his plane sixty miles off the German coast. The crew clambered into the rubber dinghies as "Weary Willie" disappeared beneath the waves, and there they drifted for thirty-eight hours, watching the glow of the fires in Hamburg, deriving some satisfaction from the roar of the RAF bombers going in for yet another attack, until they were picked up by a Danish fishing vessel. The skipper took them to the English coast, where they were met by two RAF rescue launches and taken aboard. They had survived. They would fly again. Many wouldn't. That afternoon of 25 July 140 American airmen were lost, of whom 104 became prisoners-of-war. Fifteen B-17s had been shot down and most of the rest had been damaged. It was a costly reminder to General Spatz that the US Eighth Air Force had to pay a high price for these daylight raids.

Hamburg was spared that night, save for the nuisance value of six marauding Mosquitoes. Instead, as a feint, Harris sent 600 bombers to blast Essen. That night Goebbels screamed over Radio Berlin that the English were "sadistic, brutal murderers". Privately he confided to his diary that "the last raid on Essen caused a complete stoppage in the Krupp Works".[1] It certainly had. When Herr Doktor Gustav Krupp von Bohlen und Halbach went to view his works, he collapsed with shock and fell into a coma from which he never recovered.

While the men of Bomber Command slept, the Fortresses struck at Hamburg again—300 of them, sent out from their bases in East

Anglia. But an exceptionally high number of them turned back—magneto defective, oxygen supply not working, etc, etc. The crews were showing the usual signs of a fall in morale, due to the heavy losses of the previous day.

For those who pressed on, the opposition was as intense as before, as one American navigator recalled:

> There was a terrific explosion overhead and the ship rocked badly. A second later the top turret gunner fell through the hatch and slumped to the floor. . . . When I got to him, I saw that his left arm had been blown off at the shoulder and he was a mass of blood. I first tried to inject some morphine but the needle was bent and I couldn't get it in. Then I tried to apply a tourniquet but it was impossible as the arm was off too close to the shoulder. I knew he had to have the right kind of medical treatment as soon as possible and we had four hours of flying time ahead of us so there was no alternative.
>
> I opened the escape hatch and adjusted the chute for him and placed the ripcord firmly in his right hand. But he must have become excited because he pulled the cord, opening the pilot chute in the updraft. I managed to get it together and tuck it under his right arm and toppled him into space. . . . We were 24,500 feet about twenty-five miles west of Hanover. Our only hope was that he was found and given medical attention immediately.[2]

No one knows what happened to that injured gunner. But the likelihood is that he died—either of his wounds or at the hands of local villagers. As the bombing intensified, many who baled out were killed before police or soldiers could reach them.

Of the fifty-seven bombers which did press home their attack on Hamburg, only two were shot down over the target. This time the Eighth struck lucky. Their bombs knocked out the main power station and left most of Hamburg without light or heating. Yet again, however, their "precision bombing" left much to be desired, for their bombs caused serious casualties among civilians. Forty women working in a synthetic fats factory suffered a ghastly death when the plant was hit and they were swamped in burning fat.

Up above, a B-17 flew on, swaying from side to side, so that observers in other planes thought the pilot was taking violent evasive action. In fact the pilot was dying at the controls, the top turret gunner had been dropped out of the plane and four other members of the crew were unconscious and suffering from severe frostbite. Only the navigator was unhurt. At the controls crouched the wounded co-pilot, John C. Morgan. With one hand he held onto the stick; with the other he attempted to support the pilot, the back of whose head had been blown off by a 20mm shell. But in spite of the odds against him, the young pilot brought the machine back to base, for which he received America's highest award, the Congressional Medal of Honor.

At one in the morning of Wednesday, 28 July, the Battle of Hamburg reached its climax. This time the 700-odd RAF bombers stayed for a mere forty-three minutes. But in that time they caused chaos and destruction of a kind never experienced before. The new attack was concentrated on the working-class area of Billwerder. This was nearly three miles from the aiming point worked out back in the UK, but they could not have picked a better spot to implement Bomber Harris's theory of "de-housing". Billwerder-Moorfleet, which ran along the main line from Hamburg to Berlin, was a densely crowded district of poor quality flats. Before the Nazi take-over in 1933 the Socialist trade unions had built great blocks of flats here, and here too, ironically enough, the Socialist and Communist Parties had found their strongest support in the fight against Hitler.

Now the full weight of Bomber Command's incendiaries and high explosive bombs descended upon them. "It looked like the end of the world," one flak gunner commented, as Billwerder and the neighbouring suburbs of Borgfelde and Hamm, again both working-class districts, started to burn at once. Hamburg had burned before, of course. But this was conflagration on a scale such as no one had ever seen.

Because there was hardly any wind, the flames shot upwards at tremendous speed, spreading from floor to floor and flat to flat. Within minutes whole tenement buildings on all sides were burning furiously. By the time the incendiary attack was halfway through, two out of three buildings in an area of six square miles were ablaze.

Fuelled by all the cheap furniture packed into the tenements, the inferno now started to create its own wind. The heat from a fire rises quickly, creating draughts of hot air. Fresh oxygen is required to replace that which the flame burns. As a result the air below starts to feed the flames. This is what happened in Hamburg.

The temperature soared, reaching an unprecedented 1,000 degrees Centigrade. In an instant a human body could be reduced to a handful of dust. Buildings were gutted in a flash.

157

Else Wendel had fled the shelter with her mother, but it was almost as bad outside. "It was like a furnace," she said. They had doused themselves with water against the flames, but "smoke seeped through the wet coats and began to choke us." Now they lost all sense of direction. Twisting and turning to escape the flames, they ran this way and that through blazing streets where bodies lay smouldering. Finally they found a sheltered corner, "a small green place", and collapsed in exhaustion. But not for long. Moments later they were roused by an old man crying, "*The fire is catching up with us!*"[3]

By this time the heat was so intense that it was causing new fires to start up spontaneously. First the paint on the surface of the wood bubbled and burst; then the wood itself exploded into flame. Balls of fire were constantly leaping up from places quite untouched by the incendiaries, while the uppermost reaches of the superheated fires created a central column of burning gases which matched the fiery maelstrom of the most terrible volcano ever recorded.

The wind by now had risen to a howling gale, driving a sheet of flame in front of it a quarter of a mile in diameter. This gale sent fantastic horizontal streams of fire along the streets, down the alleys, in and out of the ruins. Even the RAF bomber crews, hardened after three years of war to seeing great cities going up in flames, were aware that something unprecedented was happening below. "There were people down there being fried to death in melted asphalt on the roads, they were being burnt up and we were shuffling incendiary bombs into this holocaust," remembered Sergeant Air Gunner Geoff Parnell. "I felt terribly sorry for the people in that fire I was helping to stoke up."[4]

Later the city's Chief Medical Examiner reported:

> The dead usually lay with their faces towards the ground. Many were lying in rows. . . . Every possibility of escaping the "firestorm" behind rubble or remaining walls or corners was kept in mind. This was evident by the number of corpses found behind these ledges and corners. . . . The only safe refuge in all this time was the waters of the canals and the port. Most of those who got there were exhausted. Lips, mouth and throat were dry. They were blistered on the nose and ears, on the hands and face and their eyes burned with pain. . . . Many collapsed, then lost consciousness and died. Many jumped in the water, but even there the heat was unbearable. They took blankets and handkerchiefs, and soaked them in water. But the

water evaporated so quickly that they had to repeat the procedure every few minutes.[5]

But the Medical Examiner's report did not reflect the true horror of the firestorm. It did not mention the *Brandbomben schrumpfleichen*, "shrunken bodies of the incendiary bombs"—bodies fried to a crisp; bodies which had become charred, shrunken meat lumps; bodies burnt and fused to the nearest metal object; bodies which continued to burn whenever they were exposed to oxygen again.

For these latter had been sprayed with phosphorus from the British incendiaries. The bombs were deliberately intended to attack German morale. It is one thing to fight and douse an incendiary; it is quite another when the bomb persists in igniting again and again. And phosphorus sticks like glue to any surface it touches, whether wood, metal, concrete or human flesh.

Those who had been hit by the phosphorus ran stumbling and screaming in panic for water, any body of water in which they could immerse themselves. Many headed for the Binnenalster, the city's central lake, not far from the burning central railway station. They plunged into the lake and thrashed around in agony, knowing that the water was the only thing that would keep them from burning alive. As the bombs kept crashing down and the firestorm swept through the city, they remained there, those with phosphorus on their faces ducking and then coming up spluttering to begin burning again, halfway between death by drowning and death by burning.

Others, standing there up to their necks in water, waiting for help to arrive and put them out of their misery, found their skin was beginning to peel off. The burns festered. Thick pus oozed out. Blisters burst to expose the raw flesh below. Some couldn't take the strain. They went mad. Others slipped beneath the water to drown.

Finally the police and soldiers sealed off the whole Binnenalster and armed troops were sent in in rowing boats to deal with those for whom there was no help. Shot after shot rang out as these poor unfortunates were given what the Germans called the *Gnadenschuss*—the "shot of grace"—a bullet in the base of the skull. Then the lake was left to the dead.

The terrified men and women of Hamburg began to flee the city in their thousands. All public transport had stopped. There were no trams, tubes, trains or buses. As Frau Mathilde Wolff-Moenckeberg wrote to her daughter in Wales:

> Most people loaded some belongings on carts, bicycles, prams or carried things on their backs and started on foot, just to get away, to escape. A long stream of human beings flooded along the Sierichstrasse, thousands were prepared to camp out, anything rather than stay in this catastrophic inferno in the city. During the night the suburbs of Hamm, Hammerbrock, Rothenburgsort and Barmbeck had been almost razed to the ground. People who had fled from collapsing bunkers and had got stuck in huge crowds in the streets, had burning phosphorus poured over them, rushed into the next air-raid shelter and were shot in order not to spread the flames. In the midst of the fire and the attempts to quench it, women had their babies in the streets. Parents and children were separated and torn apart in this frightful upheaval of surging humanity and never found each other again. It must have been indescribably gruesome. Everyone had just one thought—to get away![6]

Fifteen miles away at Reinbek, a pretty little dormitory village of villas and large houses owned by rich Hamburg merchants, the locals had seen Hamburg burn for three days on the horizon. Now they watched in silence, broken only by hesitant offers of water and food, as the long procession of ashen-faced men, women and children filed by them heading for the country beyond. Irma Krueger, fifteen years old, later recalled:

> There were women, still in their night dresses and barefoot. Children wandering aimlessly without parents. Half-naked women pushing prams, also without shoes, seeming not to notice the hard cobbles of the Hamburgerstrasse. Thousands upon thousands of them, a procession of absolute misery, just trudging on and on, appearing not to see anything to left and right of them.[7]

Those who were forced to remain behind now turned their anger on the Party and its representatives. Wherever people came together to fetch water or eat a bowl of soup from the "goulash cannon", the mobile field kitchens, they vented their rage at the Nazis who had brought this terrible fate upon them. As Frau Wolff-Moenckeberg wrote: "People who wore party badges had them torn off their coats and there were screams of 'Let's get that murderer!' The police did nothing."[8]

But the police themselves were as shocked by the horrors they had seen and the terrible things they had undergone as the general populace. As the Police President of Hamburg wrote in his official report at the end of the Battle of Hamburg:

> Eyewitnesses were unable to report without succumbing to their nerves and weeping hysterically. They would try to speak, then would break down and cry, "I can't stand seeing it again. I can't stand it!". . . . Speech is impotent to portray the measure of the horror which shook the people for ten days and nights and the traces of which were written indelibly on the face of the city and its inhabitants.[9]

And still the Battle of Hamburg went on. There were six raids in all, in a period of ten days. Harris launched his final attack on the night of 2/3 August. This time the assault force of 740 bombers was to strike the upper-class districts of Harvestehude and Rothenbaum, not far from the Binnenalster, an area of fine white-stuccoed nineteenth-century mansions, where today the consulates of Britain and America stand.

However, this time the weather was against the attackers. Over the North Sea they encountered the worst electrical storm the veterans had ever witnessed. It caused over a hundred pilots to jettison their bombs into the water. A further hundred dropped their cargo of death at random, their bombs landing on several small towns within a twenty-mile radius of the stricken city, killing refugees who thought that they were finally in safety. Some 400 pilots later claimed to have dropped their bombs on Hamburg itself. But the price they paid for having done so was high. Thirty bombers were shot down, another five were lost to flak or crashed elsewhere and fifty-one were damaged. Thus nearly one fifth of the force which actually reached Hamburg was destroyed or damaged. A very high price to pay for limited success.

Below, however, they neither knew nor cared about the sufferings of the young men who had ruined their city. Else Wendel and her mother were among the survivors that morning. Like so many others they had fled to the city outskirts to escape the flames. Now the bombing was over they headed back into Hamburg, stunned by the awful scenes that met their eyes. At one stage they saw police and soldiers loading piles of charred, unrecognizable corpses onto trucks, the pitiful remains of the firestorm's victims. A women nearby told them, "I heard scream after scream. I shall never forget those screams. If there were a God, he would have shown some mercy to them. He would have helped us."

But an elderly man overheard her and said, "Leave God out of this. Men make war, not God."[10]

ENVOI

For Johnny

Do not despair
For Johnny head-in-air;
He sleeps as sound
As Johnny underground.

Fetch out no shroud
For Johnny-in-the-cloud;
And keep your tears
For him in after years.

Better by far
For Johnny-the-bright-star
To keep your head
And see his children fed.

John Pudney.

"A city of a million inhabitants has been destroyed in a manner unparalleled in history," Goebbels wrote in his diary when it was all over. "We are faced with problems that are almost impossible of solution. Food must be found. Shelter must be secured. The people must be evacuated as far as possible. They must be given clothing. In short, we are facing problems there of which we had no conception even a few weeks ago."[1]

Goebbels never did discover the full extent of the damage and destruction wrought in Hamburg, for it was only after the war that the authorities, German and Anglo-American, could assess the result of the ten-day-long assault on Hamburg.

Since 24 July Bomber Harris's men had flown 3,095 sorties and dropped 9,000 tons of high explosive and incendiaries on the city, for the loss of 86 aircraft. Over 40,000 civilians had been killed and another 37,000 had been injured. Of the dead, twelve per cent were children. A million refugees had fled the city. *In a single week, Bomber Command had killed more people than the Luftwaffe had in eight months of the blitz on England during 1940–41.* Harris had kept the grim promise he had made on the Air Ministry roof that night.

The de-housing policy advocated by Lord Cherwell had paid tremendous dividends, with fifty-four per cent of Hamburg's dwellings being destroyed. The effect on morale was devastating, as Harris had always predicted it would be. Production fell dramatically; for example, out of a work force of 9,400 at Blohm & Voss, only 300 men attended work, and elsewhere the average drop in attendance was over fifty per cent. In the streets people openly cursed Hitler and the Party, crying "We want the war to finish!"[2]

The blow to morale caused by the assault on Hamburg was experienced not only among ordinary men and women; it was felt at the very top too. As General Galland said in Berlin, "What happened in Hamburg yesterday can happen to us today" and "in spite of the strictest reticence in the official communiqués" the news of Hamburg's fate caused terror all over the Reich:

> Psychologically the war at that moment had perhaps reached its most critical point. Stalingrad had been worse, but Hamburg was not hundreds of miles away on the Volga, but on the Elbe, right in the heart of Germany.
> After Hamburg in the wide circle of political and military command could be heard the words: "The war is lost."[3]

Speer felt the same. "My reaction was that a few more of those attacks and we would be defeated," he wrote later.[4] If three or four more cities like Hamburg were destroyed, Germany's war industry would cease—not to mention the effect on public morale. And Speer said as much to Hitler.

But Hitler would not have it. Living in his remote East Prussian headquarters, surrounded by toadies and yes-men, he shared none of his people's sufferings or daily worries due to the war. In London, by contrast, Churchill lived in the front line. Twice during the blitz on London he had narrowly missed being hit by a bomb. He knew just how his people lived their daily lives during the struggle, although pre-war he had not even been on the Tube.

Hitler told Speer, "You will straighten it out as you always did before."[5] He then summoned Goering and demanded a more aggressive response from the Luftwaffe. Goering tried to persuade him that the time for that was over; if Germany were to survive, he told Hitler, she would have to adopt more defensive tactics in the west. But even Goering failed to get through to the Führer.

Shortly after this abortive interview, Galland and Peltz were called in to see their chief:

> Goering had completely broken down. His head buried in his arm on the table, he moaned some indistinguishable words. We stood there for some time in embarrassment. At last Goering pulled himself together and said we were witnessing his deepest moments of despair. The Führer had lost faith in him.[6]

Hitler had told Goering he was giving the Luftwaffe one last chance to redeem itself. He wanted renewed attacks on England—but on a bigger scale than before. "As always, the motto was *'Attack!'*" wrote Galland later. "Terror could only be smashed by counter-terror."[7]

At last Goering pulled himself together and told the Luftwaffe generals that the Führer was always right. He, Goering, had been wrong.

> All our strength was now to be concentrated on dealing to the enemy in the West such mighty retaliation blows from the air that he would not risk a second Hamburg. As a first measure in the execution of this plan, the Führer had ordered the creation of a leader of the attacks on England.[8]

Goering rose to his feet and stared at his staff officers, his cheeks turning pink with emotion. "Oberst Peltz," he cried, "I herewith appoint you Assault Leader against England!"[9]

So the war of terror in the air continued. Oberst Peltz, energetic as he was, could do little in the way of retaliation in the year that followed, while Harris's men wiped out one German city after another. But by the summer of 1944 the ultimate retaliation weapon, the V-1 or "doodlebug", was already beginning to smash down indiscriminately on London and southern England. In

February, 1945, Anglo-American bombers brought death to at least 100,000 in Dresden (some estimates, probably escalated by the so-called German Democratic Republic as anti-American propaganda, put the figure at 300,000). From Dresden it was a small step to Hiroshima, where 80,000 died, and Nagasaki, with 35,000 people killed. Indiscriminate bombing of civilian targets had become the order of the day. Back in 1940–41, Nazi Germany had indeed sown the wind.

On the German side no one spoke out publicly against this new form of terror warfare. It is not easy to speak one's mind in a police state and throughout history Germans have been noticeably lacking in what they themselves call "Zivilcourage".[10] In Britain, even in the heat of battle, there were a few who dared go against the popular tide and oppose the RAF's de-housing policy—people such as Bishop Bell of Chichester or Richard Stokes MP. There was even an opponent of the strategy at Bomber Command in the shape of the Chaplain, Rev John Collins, the future Canon Collins, co-founder of the CND movement. It was he who invited the Socialist Sir Stafford Cripps to give a talk at High Wycombe on the unlikely theme of "Is God My Co-Pilot?" The talk enraged Harris and his staff officers.

But such people were in a minority. The nation as a whole *demanded* revenge for what had happened to Britain's major cities in the early years of the war, and for those which had suffered during the Baedeker raids of 1942 and the tip-and-run attacks of 1943. In those dreadful years when Britain was being defeated on every front and blitzed day and night, Harris's men were hailed as heroes.

When peace came in 1945, however, and with it a Socialist Government promising a "brave new world", there was a disturbing change in attitude. The morality of the bombing campaign against Germany was questioned, especially by those in power. Harris and his brave young men—56,000 of whom died in battle—were denied the accolades of victory. When Harris asked for a special campaign medal for his aircrews, the request was turned down. Instead his men were offered the Defence Medal, the same decoration which was awarded to teenage fire-watchers and elderly Home Guards, who had never heard a shot fired in anger throughout the war.

Undoubtedly people were shocked by newsreel pictures of the appalling devastation wreaked on Germany's cities by the RAF and the US Eighth Air Force. Even some pilots were. When Leonard Cheshire, VC, visited Germany in 1945, he reported:

> Cologne depressed me even more than Berlin. The devastation, the cold and the despair on people's faces helped me to grasp for the first time what saturation bombing meant—to the victims. Piloting a bomber was a cold, impersonal game. We were concerned with switches and markers and flak, not with life and death. Now I understand the other side of the problem.[11]

Forty-odd years later the survivors of those "Brylcreem Boys", as the Army called them enviously, now old and white-haired, must wonder what it was all for—all that courage and self-sacrifice. Had they really gone forth every night from those remote, mud-bound airfields to bomb innocent civilians in Germany? What made them do it? And what, if anything, had they achieved?

Those who remember the Baedeker raids must feel the same. In York, Canterbury, Norwich and the like, crowded these days with millions of tourists from all over the world—including many from Germany—there is little trace of what happened that terrible spring and summer so long ago. A ruined church in the centre of York, a line of graves in Bath—not much more. It is little different at Lübeck, Cologne and Hamburg, though the massed graves in Hamburg at Ohlsdorf Main Cemetery mark the destruction of whole suburbs and their populations—Rothenburgsort, Weddel, Horn; district after district reaching right up to the solemn white mausoleum.

Back in May, 1942, three thousand people attended a memorial service in the Minster for the dead of the York Baedeker raid. Then the Dean, the Very Rev Milner White, who had himself won the DSO for bravery in the First World War, told the congregation: "On that moonlit morning, dawning red before dawn was due, York paid its toll in the defence of our England, our liberty, our race. We do not grudge it. We have not complained. We will be proud of it." And one day, he continued, looking around that vast throng:

> We shall raise a memorial over our dead, for God forbid that they should be forgotten. It will be a new sort of memorial. We are used to the records of sailors and soldiers. . . . These were the aged—so the inscription might run, "who died for the

167

children they would never see; these the fathers and mothers, who saved and hallowed England's homes under the ruins of their own; these the children who gave their years and lovely promise that freedom might play in our streets. . . . We remember you, our dead."[12]

But the memorial the Dean promised that day was never erected. When Britain concluded the war victoriously three years later, it was already clear that the character of her people was changing.

The respect for that particular kind of British past to which the Dean had alluded was already beginning to vanish. Total war had had its effect. The men and women who had fought the war at the front and in the factory no longer seemed to want, as the Dean had expressed it, to go back into "the front line of the world". The "Little England" mentality was being born.

Something vital had been eroded. One year after the Baedeker raids, teachers at the City of Bath Girls' School tried to get their pupils to write about their experiences during the two blitzes. But the girls, like their elders, were just not interested. As the school magazine complained, there was "a prevailing atmosphere of boredom" with the subject. It was the same nationwide. Indeed, those who had survived were not particularly interested in the future, and definitely not in the past, solely in the present. No one seemed particularly concerned about the fate of those who had given "their years and lovely promise". The comradeship and high purpose of that terrible time were soon forgotten.

All that remains is the long-abandoned airfield in Yorkshire or East Anglia. The Nissen huts are rusting now and in ruins. Contractors have stolen the bricks of the old control tower. Weeds and nettles have overgrown the runway. The hardstand has disappeared under brambles. Indeed, it is hard to discern that this was once an airfield at all. Was this really one of the places where Halifaxes and Lancasters once took off in their scores?

Walk through those ghostly airfields—Tockwith, Marston Moor, Holme-on-Spalding Moor or any of a dozen of those remote places—in the fading light of a late autumn afternoon, with the "sea rook" rolling in from the Yorkshire coast, and perhaps your ear might catch a faint echo of that time long ago. The scratchy sound of a battered seventy-eight, played on a wind-up gramophone: "*South of the border, down Mexico way . . .*" The harsh metallic rasp of the tannoy system system: "All crews will now report to flight . . ." The happy middle-class voice shouting, "Come on, chaps, Naafi up!"

Or perhaps you'll sense that all-pervading odour of the time, a mixture of damp greatcoats from the constant drizzle, engine oil and kerosine, the warm cheering smell of bacon and eggs frying, the cheap "Soir-de-Paris" scent that the WAAFs in the cookhouse favoured.

Is it just a trick of the grey wavering light, the fog slipping silently in and out of the ruins? Yes, it must be. Those silent, bulky shapes, padding out noiselessly across the field where the damp steaming sheep now graze, they must surely be a figment of your imagination. After all, those brave young men have been dead for over forty years. Yet among those abandoned huts, with a smashed door creaking eerily in the faint breeze from the sea, gazing down the cracked, overgrown runway, it is not so difficult to visualize them clambering into "C for Charlie", hugging their lucky charms, heading for the horrors of Flak Alley yet again.

Back in York in 1942, after the Baedeker raid on the city, it was proposed that the big clock outside the church of St Martin-le-Grand, which had been wrecked in the bombing (it is still a shell to this day, much admired and photographed by the sons and grandsons of those who wrecked it over four decades ago), should be kept permanently stopped at the time it ceased to beat—three forty-five am on the morning of 29 April, 1942.

It was reasoned that this stopped clock in the centre of York's principal street, Coney Street, would be a permanent reminder to all, local and stranger alike, of what had once happened to the ancient northern city that night. But in the heat and confusion of total war, the proposal was forgotten and after the war the big clock was duly repaired. Now it has been ticking away these forty years or more, the fate of the church to which it is still attached long forgotten. And perhaps it is right that it does. For in a way, the clock is a symbol that time in that terrible spring of 1942 didn't stop after all.

BIBLIOGRAPHY

Bowyer, Michael: *Air Raid* (Patrick Stephens, Wellingborough 1986)
Boyle, Andrew: *No Passing Glory* (Collins, London 1957)
Caidin, M.: *The Night Hamburg Died* (Four Square, London 1960)
Calder, Angus: *The People's War* (Cape, London 1969)
Cassandra (William Connor): *The English At War* (Secker and Warburg, London 1942)
Cheshire, Leonard: *Bomber Pilot* (Hutchinson, London 1943)
Churchill, Winston: *Great War Speeches* (Corgi, London 1957)
Clarke, C.: *If The Nazis Had Come* (World Distributors, London 1961)
Collier, Richard: *1940: The World in Flames* (Penguin 1963)
Dickens, A. G.: *Lübeck Diary* (Gollancz, London 1947)
Evans, R.: *On The Other Side* (Pan 1984)
Flowers, D.: *The Taste of Courage* (Harper & Row, New York 1961)
Fowles, John: *Daniel Martin* (Granada 1979)
Galland, Adolf: *The First and The Last: The German Fighter Forces in World War II* (London 1955)
Goebbels, Josef: *Tagebucher* (Berthelsmann, Gutersloh 1976)
Hamilton, Nigel: *Montgomery* (Coronet 1985)
Hastings, Max: *Bomber Command* (Michael Joseph 1979)
Hodson, James Lansdale: *Home Front* (Gollancz, London 1944)
Jones, R. V.: *Most Secret War* (Hamish Hamilton, London 1978)
Longmate, Norman: *The Bombers* (Hutchinson, London 1983)
————: *The GIs* (Hutchinson, London 1975)
Lucas, Laddie: *Out Of The Blue* (Hutchinson, London 1985)
McLaine, Ian: *Ministry of Morale* (Allen & Unwin, London 1979)
Mosley, Leonard: *London Under Fire* (Pan, London 1971)
Pile, Frederick: *Ack-Ack* (Harrap, London 1949)
Rawnsley, C. F., and Wright, Robert: *Night Fighter* (Corgi 1957)
Rootes, A.: *Front-Line County* (Robert Hale, London 1980)
Rothnie, N.: *The Bombing of Bath* (Ashgrove Press, Bath 1983)

Saward, Dudley: *"Bomber" Harris* (Buchan & Enright, London 1984)

Schreiber, A.: *Als von Himmel Feuer Fiel* (Lübecker Nachrichten, Lübeck 1982)

Speer, Albert: *Inside the Third Reich* (Weidenfeld & Nicolson, London 1970)

Swain, George: *Norwich Under Fire* (Jarrold & Son, Norwich 1945)

Taylor, E.: *1,000 Bomber Raid* (Robert Hale, London 1987)

SOURCES AND NOTES

Introduction
1. Four years later I was a student at the patched up and partially rebuilt University of Cologne.
2. Quoted in *Sunday Telegraph*, 17 August, 1986.

Part One: Chapter 1
1. *Patentanten:* "god-aunts", the German equivalent of godparents.
2. Personal interview.
3. Ibid.
4. Ibid.
5. Schreiber, *Als von Himmel Feuer Fiel* (author's translation).
6. Quoted in Flowers, *The Taste of Courage*.
7. Personal interview.
8. Quoted in Schreiber, op. cit.
9. Ibid.
10. Ibid.
11. Dickens, *Lübeck Diary*.
12. Quoted in Schreiber, op. cit.
13. Ibid.
14. Ibid.
15. Goebbels, *Tagebucher*.
16. Ibid.

Chapter 2
1. Quoted in Collier, *1940: The World in Flames*.
2. Quoted in Hastings, *Bomber Command*.
3. Ibid.
4. Ibid.
5. Ibid.
6. Quoted in Hodson, *Home Front*.

7. Quoted in Hastings, op. cit.
8. Personal interview with Flight Lieutenant John Watson, a Scot who later won the DFC.
9. Quoted in Longmate, *The Bombers*.
10. Goebbels, *Tagebucher*.
11. Quoted in Calder, *The People's War*.
12. From *Meldungen aus dem Reich* (Luchterhand, Neuwied 1965).
13. Quoted in Hastings, op. cit.
14. Pile, *Ack-Ack*.
15. Ibid.
16. Ibid.
17. Ibid.

Chapter 3
1. Cassandra, *The English At War*.
2. Ibid.
3. Quoted in Clarke, *If The Nazis Had Come*.
4. It was the Americans who named the system "radar" and the name soon caught on everywhere, even in Germany.
5. Rawnsley and Wright, *Night Fighter*.
6. Ibid.
7. Jones, *Most Secret War*.
8. Ibid.
9. Ibid.
10. Fowles, *Daniel Martin*.
11. Until the National Fire Service was formed there had been 1,600 different local fire brigades, each with its own equipment—which was not always compatible with the neighbouring area's equipment. As a result, the hoses of visiting firemen called in to help tackle a blaze often did not fit the local fire hydrant, and the outside firemen were forced to stand by helplessly as properties burned down.
12. Rawnsley and Wright, op. cit.
13. Ibid.
14. It is difficult to assess the casualties in Exeter after this first raid because of the other raids that followed almost immediately after it, before the city's authorities had time to collect themselves.
15. Hodson, *Home Front*.
16. Goebbels, op. cit.
17. Ibid.

Chapter 4
1. During the war, for obvious reasons, there were no public weather forecasts, either over the radio or in the press.
2. Quoted in *Bath and Western Chronicle*, 18 April, 1982.
3. *Leben wie Gott in Frankreich* was the German equivalent of "live the life of Riley".

4. *Völkischer Beobachter*, 26 April, 1942.
5. Ibid.
6. Ibid.
7. Quoted in Rothnie, *The Bombing of Bath*.
8. *Bath and Western Chronicle*, loc. cit.
9. Quoted in Rothnie, op. cit.
10. *Völkischer Beobachter*, loc. cit.
11. Quoted in *Bath and Western Chronicle*, loc. cit.
12. Goebbels, op. cit.
13. Quoted in Rothnie, op. cit.
14. Ibid.
15. Ibid.
16. Ibid.
17. Ibid.
18. *Western Daily Press*, 26 April, 1942.
19. Quoted in Rothnie, op. cit.

Chapter 5
1. Quoted in Pile, *Ack-Ack*.
2. Ibid.
3. In 1940, for example, the Germans used the code numbers 51, 52 and 53 respectively for Wolverhampton, Birmingham and Coventry. That same year the code word for an attack on Birmingham was "Umbrella"—easy enough to decipher for the umbrella was associated with the then Prime Minister, Neville Chamberlain, and he in turn was closely associated with Birmingham.
4. Pile, op. cit.
5. Jones, *Most Secret War*.
6. Quoted in *Bath and Western Chronicle*, 18 April, 1982.
7. Quoted in Rothnie, *The Bombing of Bath*.
8. Ibid.
9. Ibid.
10. Ibid.
11. Quoted in Schreiber, *Als von Himmel Feuer Fiel*.
12. Goebbels, op. cit.
13. Ibid.
14. Ibid.
15. Quoted in Hastings, *Bomber Command*.
16. Ibid.
17. Ibid.
18. Personal communication to author.
19. Quoted in Hastings, op. cit.
20. Ibid.
21. Ibid.
22. Ibid.

Chapter 6
1. Personal communication to author.
2. Swain, *Norwich Under Fire*.
3. This was certainly proven to be true in Hull in 1941, when whole lines of brick-built shelters in the streets were flattened by bomb blast.
4. Quoted in *Eastern Counties Newspapers*, 14 April, 1967.
5. Personal communication.
6. Quoted in *Eastern Counties Newspapers*, 14 April, 1967.
7. Swain, op. cit.
8. Personal communication.
9. Quoted in Bowyer, *Air Raid*.
10. Quoted in *Eastern Counties Newspapers*, 30 April, 1942.
11. Ibid.
12. Ibid.
13. Bowyer, op. cit.
14. Ibid.
15. Ibid.
16. Swain, op. cit.
17. Quoted in Bowyer, op. cit.
18. Quoted in *Eastern Counties Newspapers*, 14 April, 1967.
19. Ibid.
20. Ibid.
21. Personal communication.
22. Ibid.

Chapter 7
1. Swain, *Norwich Under Fire*.
2. Quoted in Bowyer, *Air Raid*.
3. *Eastern Counties Newspapers*, 30 April, 1942.
4. Ibid.
5. Rotenburg's fate would be sealed not by bombs but by artillery shells towards the end of the war.
6. Quoted in *Eastern Counties Newspapers*, 14 April, 1967.
7. Swain, op. cit.
8. Ibid.
9. Quoted in *Eastern Counties Newspapers*, 14 April, 1967.
10. Quoted in McLaine, *Ministry of Morale*.
11. Ibid.
12. Ibid.
13. Quoted in Longmate, *The Bombers*.
14. Ibid.
15. *Norwich Mercury*, April, 1942.

Part Two: Chapter 1
1. Quoted in Lucas, *Out of the Blue*.
2. Ibid.

3. *Yorkshire Evening Press*, 28 April, 1942.
4. Personal communication.
5. Personal communication.
6. Personal communication.
7. *Yorkshire Evening Press*, 28 April, 1942.
8. Ibid.
9. Personal communication.
10. Personal communication.
11. Personal communication.
12. *Yorkshire Evening Press*, 29 April, 1942.
13. Personal communication.
14. Personal communication.
15. Ibid.
16. *Yorkshire Evening Press*, 28 April, 1942.
17. Ibid.

Chapter 2
1. *Yorkshire Post* and *Yorkshire Evening Press*, 29 April, 1942.
2. *Yorkshire Evening Press*, 29 April, 1942.
3. Ibid.
4. Ibid.
5. Personal communication to author.
6. Ibid.
7. *Yorkshire Evening Press*, 29 April, 1942.
8. Ibid.
9. Ibid.
10. Personal communication to author.
11. Ibid.
12. *Norwich Mercury*, 30 April, 1942.
13. Quoted in Hodson, *Home Front*.
14. Ibid.
15. Ibid.
16. Quoted in Boyle, *No Passing Glory*.
17. Personal communication to author.
18. Quoted in Boyle, op. cit.
19. Quoted in Exeter's *Express and Echo*, 5 May, 1942.
20. Ibid.
21. Ibid.
22. Ibid.
23. Ibid.
24. Ibid.
25. Quoted in *Daily Telegraph*, 5 May, 1942.
26. *Sydney Sun*, May, 1942.

Chapter 3
1. Churchill, *Great War Speeches*.
2. Ibid.

3. Hodson, *Home Front*.
4. Ibid.
5. Quoted in Hamilton, *Montgomery* (vol 2).
6. Quoted in Hastings, *Bomber Command*.
7. Ibid.
8. Ibid.
9. Quoted in Saward, *"Bomber" Harris*.
10. Ibid.
11. Personal communication to author.
12. Quoted in Hastings, op. cit.
13. Bowyer, *Air Raid*.
14. Personal communication.
15. Personal communication.
16. Personal communication.

Chapter 4
1. Personal communication.
2. The air-raid shelters built in Germany were massive pre-stressed concrete affairs, quite unlike the British ones. Even after the war they resisted Allied attempts to blow them up, and can still be seen in most large German cities today—lasting monuments to the Third Reich.
3. Personal communication.
4. Personal communication.
5. Personal communication.
6. Quoted in Taylor, *1,000 Bomber Raid*.
7. Ibid.
8. Ibid.
9. Ibid.
10.. Speer, *Inside the Third Reich*.
11. Ibid.
12. Ibid.
13. Quoted in Hastings, *Bomber Command*.
14. Ibid.
15. Quoted in McLaine, *Ministry of Morale*.
16. Ibid.
17. Quoted in *Daily Telegraph*, 1 June, 1942.
18. Quoted in Taylor, op. cit.
19. Quoted in Hastings, op. cit.

Chapter 5
1. Quoted in Calder, *The People's War*.
2. Quoted in Hastings, *Bomber Command*.
3. Personal communication.
4. *Kentish Gazette*, 28 May, 1942.
5. Personal communication.
6. *Kentish Gazette*, op. cit.
7. Personal communication.

8. Ibid.
9. *Kentish Gazette*, op. cit.
10. *Völkischer Beobachter*, 1 June, 1942.
11. Quoted in Rootes, *Front Line County*.
12. Personal communication.
13. *Kentish Gazette*, 28 May, 1942.
14. Rootes, op. cit.
15. Did this "confidential information" mean that the Germans had a high-ranking mole in the ranks of the Church of England? For the fact is that this entry in Goebbels's diary is dated January, 1942–three months before Dr Temple was appointed.
16. Goebbels, op. cit.
17. *Meldungen aus dem Reich*.
18. Rootes, op. cit.
19. *Kentish Gazette*, op. cit.
20. Personal communication.
21. Ibid.
22. Anon: *Front-line School* (Jennings, Canterbury 1945).
23. *The Times*, 2 June, 1942.
24. Rootes, op. cit.
25. *Meldungen aus dem Reich*.
26. Ibid.
27. Galland, *The First and the Last*.
28. Quoted in Bowyer, *Air Raid*.
29. Pile, *Ack-Ack*.
30. Quoted in Longmate, *The Bombers*.
31. Personal communication.
32. Quoted in Longmate, *The GIs*.

Chapter 6.
1. *Daily Express*, 29 January, 1942.
2. Quoted in Longmate, *The GIs*.
3. Ibid.
4. Quoted in Hastings, *Bomber Command*.
5. Ibid.
6. Personal communication.
7. Quoted in Taylor, *1,000 Bomber Raid*.
8. Quoted in Longmate, *The GIs*.
9. Quoted in Hastings, op. cit.
10. Quoted in Longmate, *The GIs*.
11. Ibid.
12. Jones, *Most Secret War*.
13. Ibid.

Chapter 7
1. Quoted in Longmate, *The Bombers*.
2. Ibid.

3. Ibid.
4. Quoted in Flowers, *The Taste of Courage.*
5. Quoted in Evans, *On the Other Side.*
6. Quoted in Flowers, op. cit.
7. Ibid.
8. Quoted in Hastings, *Bomber Command.*
9. Ibid.
10. Saward, *"Bomber" Harris.*
11. Quoted in Longmate, op. cit.
12. Jones, *Most Secret War.*
13. Quoted in Flowers, op. cit.
14. Quoted in Evans, op. cit.
15. Quoted in Longmate, op. cit.
16. Ibid.
17. Speer, *Inside the Third Reich.*
18. Ibid.
19. Goebbels, op. cit.
20. *Meldungen aus dem Reich.*
21. Ibid.

Chapter 8
1. Goebbels, op. cit.
2. Quoted in Caidin, *The Night Hamburg Died.*
3. Quoted in Flowers, *The Taste of Courage.*
4. Quoted in Longmate, *The Bombers.*
5. Quoted in Caidin, op. cit.
6. Quoted in Evans, *On the Other Side.*
7. Personal communication.
8. Quoted in Evans, op. cit.
9. Quoted in Caidin, op. cit.
10. Quoted in Flowers, op. cit.

Envoi
1. Goebbels, op. cit.
2. Longmate, *The Bombers.*
3. Galland, *The First and the Last.*
4. Speer, *Inside the Third Reich.*
5. Ibid.
6. Galland, op. cit.
7. Ibid.
8. Ibid.
9. Ibid.
10. *Zivilcourage:* a difficult concept to translate, but perhaps the best interpretation is a mixture of personal and public-spirited bravery.
11. Cheshire, *Bomber Pilot.*
12. *Yorkshire Evening Press*, May 1942.

INDEX